Reverie and Interpretation

Other Books by Thomas Ogden

Projective Identification and Psychotherapeutic Technique

The Matrix of the Mind: Object Relations and the Psychoanalytic Dialogue

The Primitive Edge of Experience

Subjects of Analysis

Reverie and Interpretation

Sensing Something Human

THOMAS H. OGDEN, M.D.

JASON ARONSON INC.
Northvale, New Jersey
London

Certain chapters in this book are based on prior publications of the author. He gratefully acknowledges permission from the following journals to reprint this previously published material.
Chapter 2: "Analysing Forms of Aliveness and Deadness of the Transference–Countertransference," *International Journal of Psycho-Analysis*, 76:695–709, 1995 (Copyright © Institute of Psycho-Analysis).
Chapter 3: "The Perverse Subject of Analysis," *Journal of the American Psychoanalytic Association*, 44:1121–1146, 1996 (Copyright © The American Psychoanalytic Association).
Chapters 4 and 5: "Reconsidering Three Aspects of Psychoanalytic Technique," *The International Journal of Psycho-Analysis*, 77:883–899, 1996 (Copyright © Institute of Psycho-Analysis).
Chapter 6: "Reverie and Interpretation," *The Psychoanalytic Quarterly*, 66:567–595, 1997 (Copyright © The Psychoanalytic Quarterly, Inc.).
Chapter 7: "Some Thoughts on the Use of Language in Psychoanalysis," *Psychoanalytic Dialogues*, 7:1–21, 1997 (Copyright © The Analytic Press).
Chapter 8: "Listening: Three Frost Poems," *Psychoanalytic Dialogues*, 7:619–639, 1997 (Copyright © The Analytic Press).

The author also gratefully acknowledges permission to reprint:
– in Chapter 2, the poem from *Jorge Luis Borges Selected Poems 1923–1967* by Jorge Luis Borges. Copyright © 1968, 1969, 1970, 1971, 1972 by Jorge Luis Borges, Emece Editores, S.A. and Norman Thomas DiGiovanni. Used by permission of Delacorte Press/Seymour Lawrence, a division of Bantam Doubleday Dell Publishing Group, Inc.
– in Chapter 8, the poems from *The Poetry of Robert Frost*, edited by Edward Connery Lathem. Copyright 1941, 1942 by Robert Frost. © 1970 by Lesley Frost Ballantine. © 1969 by Henry Holt & Co., Inc. Reprinted by permission of Henry Holt & Co., Inc.

Director of Editorial Production: Robert D. Hack

This book was set in 12 pt. New Baskerville by FASTpages of Nanuet, NY.

Copyright © 1997 by Thomas H. Ogden.

10 9 8 7 6 5 4 3 2 1

Library of Congress Cataloging-in-Publication Data

Ogden, Thomas H.
    Reverie and interpretation: sensing something human / Thomas H. Ogden.
        p.   cm.
    Includes bibliographical references and index.
    ISBN 0–7657–0076–X
    1. Psychoanalysis.   2. Psychoanalytic interpretation.   I. Title.
    RC509.O33   1997
    616.89'17—dc21   97–9833

Printed in the United States of America on acid-free paper. For information and catalog write to Jason Aronson Inc., 230 Livingston Street, Northvale, New Jersey 07647-1726. Or visit our website: http://www.aronson.com

In memory of Jane Hewitt,
whose vitality and love were
so fierce and so tender
that I will never know their like again

Contents

Sitting in that chair, rocking and
gazing at the wallpaper, one seemed
to turn into a mere tangle of rising and
falling tendrils that would grow within
a couple of seconds from nothingness
to their full size and then as rapidly
disappear into themselves again.

Robert Musil, *Five Women*, 1924

1

On the Art of Psychoanalysis

Words and sentences, like people, must be allowed a certain slippage. I do not mean to suggest that words, sentences (and human beings) can be said to mean (or be) anything we wish them to mean (or be). Rather, I am drawing attention to the stifling effect on imagination of our efforts to define, to specify with ever increasing precision, what we mean (who we are). Imagination depends on the play of possibilities. In this volume, words and sentences at their best will be only loosely "fastened to the page" (Frost 1929, p. 713). I will use words such as "aliveness" and "deadness," "human" and "perverse," "sincere" and "inauthentic" without defining them except—and this is a large exception—except in the way they are used in sentences. I will at different times use the words "empty," "stagnant," "stale" and "stillborn" to talk about an experience of emotional deadness. The reader might reasonably ask, "Which of these feelings or states, if any, does Ogden have in mind when he speaks of emotional deadness? Moreover, isn't the very idea of the *experience* of emotional deadness an oxymoron?" I will ask the reader to allow me (and himself) room in which a sense of emptiness might slide into a feeling of deadness, and then into a deadness of feeling, and then back again into an experience of emptiness, picking up shadings of meaning along the way. It is important that words be used (and read) in a way that allows their accrued meanings to be altered by (and to affect) each new emotional context in which they are spoken or written or read.

It has increasingly seemed to me that the sense of aliveness and deadness of a given moment of an analytic hour is perhaps the most important gauge of the analytic process. The attempt to use language to capture/convey a sense of this delicate interplay of aliveness and deadness of human experience in the analytic setting represents a major challenge to contemporary psychoanalysis and will be a central concern of this book. Although this facet of the analytic experience will not occupy the foreground of each chapter, it is my hope that it will be felt to lie in the wings of virtually every sentence.

In attempting to capture something of the experience of being alive in words, the words themselves must be alive. Words, when they are living and breathing, are like musical chords. The full resonance of the chord or phrase must be allowed to be heard in all of its suggestive imprecision. We must attempt in our use of language, both in our theory-making and in our analytic practice, to be makers of music, rather than players of notes. To that end, we have little choice but to accept that a word or a sentence is not a still point of meaning and will not sound the same or mean the same thing a moment later. When a patient asks me to repeat what I have just said, I may tell him something to the effect that I cannot since that moment is gone. I add that he and I might try to say something that takes as its starting point his feeling about what has just occurred.

Words and sentences, like people, are forever in motion. The attempt to fix the meanings of words and sentences turns them into lifeless effigies, immobile stained cells preserved on laboratory slides that are only barely suggestive of the living tissue from which they came. When the language of analyst or analysand becomes stagnant, it is no longer of any use in the task of conveying a sense of living human experience. What I aspire to in the use of language in the analytic dialogue is captured in A.R. Ammons' (1968) comparison of living language in poetry to a walk: "A walk involves the whole person; it is not reproducible; its shape occurs, unfolds; it has a motion characteristic of the walker" (p. 118).

What it means to bring a person, a feeling, an idea, to life in writing is to be found in the *reader's experience of reading or hearing* the words and sentences being said (written) by the writer. This is the challenge of all literature and of all analytic writing since both are fundamentally concerned with the task of using language to capture something of human experience. If we as readers cannot sense something human, however faint, in the experience of reading an analytic paper, a poem, an essay, or a novel, then we come away empty-handed. The work of the analytic writer, like the writer of poetry or fiction, begins and ends with his effort to create *in* the language the experience of human alive-ness. If an analytic writer contents himself with talking "about" aliveness or deadness (that "stolid word *about*" [Wm. James 1890, p. 246]), his efforts will certainly be in vain. This book, if it is to achieve anything of its goal of capturing something of human experience in the analytic setting, must attempt at all times to be an experiment in which the writer in the act of writing and the reader in the act of reading *experiences* a sense of aliveness that exists in the language being used. This book will be of value in the sense I am describing to the extent that the reader now and again has the experi-ence of *feeling* what aliveness is in what it feels like to read the sentences, or as Frost (1962) liked to put it, "to say the lines" (p. 911).

The reader must do at least half the work in gain-ing from the language of this book a sense of what it is to be alive. "The process of reading is not a half-sleep, but, in highest sense, an exercise, a gymnast's struggle. . . . The reader is to do something for himself, must be on the alert, must himself or herself instruct indeed the poem, argument, history, metaphysical essay—the text furnishing the hints, the clue, the start or framework" (Whitman 1871, p. 992). The black and white shapes on the page and the white space that surrounds those markings are inert. The reader must do something with them. He must actively, even passionately, engage with the words in the act of using himself to create something human of his own, in his own terms. After all, what terms, other than one's own, are there with which to create an experience that is human?

Among the most astute comments concerning what it means for an analysis to be alive has come (as one might expect), not from an analyst, but from a novelist and essayist, speaking in 1884 about the art of fiction:

> The good health of an art which undertakes to reproduce life must demand that it be perfectly free. It lives upon exercise and the very meaning of exercise is freedom. The only obligation to which in advance we may hold a novel, without incurring the accusation of being arbitrary, is that it be interesting. [Henry James 1884, p. 49]

James' statement about the novel (and implicitly about the relationship of writer and reader) has important relevance to the art of psychoanalysis and to the understanding of the relationship of analyst and analysand. The idea that above all an analysis must be interesting is for me both self-evident and a revolutionary conception (cf. Phillips 1996). To be interesting, the analysis must be free to "exercise," to shape itself and be given shape in any way that the participants are able to invent. The freedom to "exercise" is the freedom to experiment: "Art lives upon discussion, upon experiment, upon curiosity, upon variety of attempt, upon the exchange of views and the comparison of standpoints" (H. James 1884, pp. 44-45). When the analysis is alive, it unselfconsciously manages for periods of time to be an experiment that has left the well charted waters of prescribed form; it is a discussion fueled by curiosity and by variety of attempt; it is an endeavor that depends upon genuine exchange of views and comparison of standpoints. Analysis that has become a routinized form in which "knowledge" is conveyed from analyst to analysand is uninteresting; it is no longer an experiment since the answers, at least in broad outline, are known from the outset. The form of a novel and of an analysis must not be pre-scribed. To do so is to foreclose experiment:

> The form, it seems to me, is to be appreciated after the fact: then the author's choice has been made . . . ; then we can follow lines and directions. . . . The execution belongs to the author alone; it is what is most personal to him, and we measure him by that. The advantage, the luxury, as well as the torment and responsibility of a novelist is that there is no limit to what he may attempt as an executant—no limit to his possible experiments, efforts, discoveries, successes. [H. James 1884, p. 50]

As is the case with the novel, the form of an analysis can only be appreciated in hindsight. For example, an analyst does not plan to play a role in a perverse scene in an analytic relationship. The "script" or form of the perverse scenario is a reflection of the analysand's internal object world and is given shape as an unconscious intersubjective construction of analyst and analysand. Understanding of the meanings of the form is almost always retrospective and this form is indeed what is most personal to its authors. We ask a great deal of ourselves as analysts and as analysands in demanding that we not rely on "pre-scribed" form, that we attempt to be open to experiment: "There is no limit [in range, intensity and complexity of feeling and thought] to what he [analyst or analysand] may attempt." Moreover, we ask of ourselves that we be unconsciously available to be subjects in the unconscious experiment of the other. We as analysts attempt to render ourselves unconsciously receptive to being made use of in playing a variety of roles in the unconscious life of the analysand. Unconscious receptivity of this sort (Bion's [1962a] state of "reverie") involves (a partial) giving over of one's separate individuality to a third subject, a subject that is neither analyst nor analysand but a third subjectivity unconsciously generated by the analytic pair (Ogden 1994a). To consistently offer oneself in this way is no small matter: it represents an emotionally draining undertaking in which analyst and analysand each to a degree "loses his mind" (his capacity to think and create experience as a distinctly separate individual).

It is only in the process of terminating an analysis that analyst and analysand "retrieve" their separate minds, but the minds "retrieved" are not the minds of the individuals who had entered into the analytic experience. Those individuals no longer exist. The analyst and analysand that are "retrieved" as separate individuals are themselves in significant ways new psychological entities having been created/changed by their experience in and of the third analytic subject ("the subject of analysis").

The analysand's experience of the death of the analyst prior to the planned ending of a fruitful analysis[1] represents not only an experience of enormous personal loss, but, as important, an experience of a type of insanity. The analyst's death forecloses for the analysand the possibility of fully retrieving his mind (a mind that has not been exclusively his own personal possession for some time). The aspect of mind that has (in part) been "lost" is the mind that has been generated and developed intersubjectively. It is a mind that can be appropriated by the analysand only gradually in the course of an uninterrupted analytic experience. The death of the analyst represents a violent disruption of "the place where [the analysand] lives" (Winnicott 1971a). The (impossible) responsibility of the analyst to stay alive for the entirety of the analysis is a heavy one and constitutes one of the strains of the profession

---

1. The idea of a "fruitful" analysis is to be differentiated from the illusory conception of a "completed" analysis that has been brought to a successful termination after the transference conflicts and distortions have been successfully "resolved."

that I think has not been sufficiently recognized. We underestimate the pressure generated by the analyst's (largely unconscious) knowledge that he (along with almost every parent) has implicitly promised what he cannot possibly guarantee—to stay alive long enough for the analysand (or child) to retrieve/create a mind of his own capable of generating a separate place in which to live that is outside of, and yet never completely separate from, the shared mental space in which he has grown up.

The art of analysis is an art form that requires not only that we struggle with the problem of creating a place where analyst and analysand might live, but also requires that we develop a use of language adequate to giving voice to our experience of what life feels like in that ever shifting place. We ask of ourselves (and of our analysands) that we attempt to speak in our own voice with our own words, for this is a very large part of what allows analysis to be a human event. "The execution belongs to the author alone; it is what is most personal to him. . . ." Paradoxically, it requires a great deal of training and experience to be able to talk in a way that feels and sounds spontaneous, unpracticed, uncontrived, undictated by analytic convention or prescription. This is not simply a matter of the analyst's growing, over the course of time, to feel more familiar with, and comfortable in, the role of analyst. An analyst at any stage of his career may come to substitute for the sound of his own voice and the choice of his own words the stale formulaic sound of "accepted" technique as

defined by an affiliation to a school of analytic thought
or by a conscious or unconscious imitation of or identification with his own analyst(s), supervisors, or other
analysts whom he currently respects and admires.

It is a very great achievement indeed for an analyst
to develop the capacity to "simply talk" to his
analysand. The idea of "simply talking" might be
thought of as the analogue to Freud's (1912) instruction to the analyst: "Simply listen" (p. 112). So often
therapists and analysts speak in a "therapeutic voice"
(parodied in an often disconcertingly accurate way in
films such as *Annie Hall* and *Sex, Lies and Video
Tape*). Such stiff therapeutic tones are like those heard
in no other form of human discourse.

Learning to talk with patients with a voice of one's
own and with words of one's own requires that one
learn to hear and to use "the *living* sounds of speech"
(Frost 1915, p. 687): "the vital thing then in all compo-
sition, in prose and verse . . . is the ACTION of the
voice. . . . Get the *stuff* of life into the technique of
your writing. That's the only escape from dry rhetoric"
(p. 688). It is also the analyst's only escape from dry
"therapeutic" rhetoric, or dead language. The analyst's
speech must be the creation of a person who is alive in
that moment. Living human speech is as difficult to
come by in the analyst's spoken use of language as it is
in written prose or verse.

Some years later, Frost (1929) expanded on the
idea of "*living* sounds of speech":

Everything written is as good as it is dramatic. . . . A dramatic necessity goes deep into the nature of the sentence. Sentences are not different enough to hold the attention unless they are dramatic. No ingenuity of varying structure will do. All that can save them is the speaking tone of voice somehow entangled in the words . . . for the ear of the imagination. [p.713]

In this passage, Frost's word "dramatic" is itself dramatic. It is a word that is unexpected and conveys a good deal of what Frost calls the "fetching" (1918, p. 694) use of everyday words, somehow transformed into newly made words (words "fetched" from their customary place). The word "dramatic" has been newly made here so that it no longer means histrionic, hysterical, shocking, flashy, glamorous, theatrical, and the like. It seems more to suggest that the language is personal, unique to the person speaking it, particular to the situation in which it is spoken and to the person to whom it is spoken. As a result, "dramatic" speech (quite the opposite of being staged) is a highly revealing and intimate use of language in that one has offered and entrusted to another person something that one has made *for him* to use as he will. It is a use of language that is risk-taking in that it asks something of the listener in the process of making something for him. In being alive and present in one's language, in having "one's speaking tone of voice somehow . . . entangled in the words," the speaker asks that an aspect of himself be recognized "by the ear of the [listener's] imagination."

To have one's attempts to speak "dramatically" (intimately and personally) go unheard and unused is no small event for either analyst or analysand. When the analyst's words go unheard, it is an isolating, frustrating and disappointing event. When the analysand's words (and the aspect of himself that is entangled in his words and speaking tone of voice) go unheard by the analyst, it is a far more serious matter: it is a reflection of the fact that the analyst, for the moment, is no longer able to provide "an imagining ear," a living human presence to be with and to be talked to. The analysand's self-protective withdrawal will almost certainly follow (for example, in the form of acting-in or acting out, somatization, reliance on manic, paranoid, and autistic defenses, and so on). Such is the nature of human discourse: a lapse of this sort on the part of the analyst is painful, but not tragic. It is part of the rhythm of analytic discourse and of all other forms of human discourse. However, if this pattern continues unabated and unexamined in an analytic setting, something far more destructive to the analysis is set in motion. When the analyst is unable to analyze the unconscious thoughts, feelings, and sensations (often manifested in the analyst's reverie experience) that are preventing him from listening freely and imaginatively, a gulf between the analyst and the analysand grows. Until this state of affairs is recognized and folded into the self-reflective work of the analysis, either through countertransference analysis, or through the patient's successfully bringing the matter to the awareness of the analyst, genuine analytic work has come to an end. Such impasses often require that the analyst seek consultation or further personal analysis.

As will be discussed in later chapters, I believe that the analytic task most fundamentally involves the effort of the analytic pair to help the analysand become human in a fuller sense than he has been able to achieve to this point. This is no abstract, philosophical quest; it is a requirement of the species as basic as the need for food and air. The effort to become human is among the very few things in a person's life that may over time come to feel more important to him than his personal survival.

Again, I will turn to a poet and playwright to provide language with which to convey a sense of the way in which the survival of the individual is quite different from *the experience* of being alive. Goethe's *Faust* (1808) is for me one of the most powerful expressions in literature of the battle for life as a human being. The complexity of *Faust* is lost when the protagonist is viewed as a man who "makes a deal with the devil" in which he trades his soul for unrestricted access to life's pleasures (many of which are "forbidden" sensual pleasures). The opening scenes of *Faust I* to my mind present a far more interesting and complex character and dilemma. We are introduced to Faust as a man who is in a state of deep despair after having devoted his life to studying "Philosophy, Law, Medicine—and what is

worst—Theology." "Yet I am a wretched fool/and still
no wiser than before." "I get no joy from anything."
"No dog would want to linger on like this."

It takes some time for the reader/audience to get a
sense of the sources of this despair. Faust has studied in
vain and has come to view God as useless to him, not
because he wants to become more than human in order
to gain access to pleasures forbidden to mortal men.
Quite the contrary. What Faust longs for is to be a mortal
man (the very thing he feels that God has denied him).
Mephistopheles fails to understand this and offers him
unending earthly delights ("You can sample whatever
you like"), but Faust is not in the least interested in the
prospect of being able to "snatch what suits [his] passing
fancy." Faust yearns not for a privileged place outside of
human experience and time, but rather seeks a place
within it: "Let's plunge into the torrents of time/into the
world of eventful experience" (p. 45). Faust goes on:

> and I'm resolved my most inmost being shall
> share in what's the lot of all mankind that I shall
> understand their heights and depths, shall fill my
> heart with all their joys and griefs, and so expand
> myself to theirs and, like them, suffer shipwreck
> too. [p. 46]

Faust feels that he has not experienced what it is to
be human ("the lot of all mankind") and uses the
words "their" and "them" in a way that reflects his feeling that he occupies a position outside of humankind.

Goethe's framing of Faust's dilemma in this way captures for me what is most basic to the therapeutic task of psychoanalysis: the effort to create conditions in which a particular type of discourse might take place in which the analysand and the analyst attempt to enhance their capacity to take part in "eventful experience," to experience a full range of "the joys and griefs, the heights and depths" of human emotion.

Although the capacity to be human in this sense is viewed by Faust as "the lot of all mankind," Faust does not yet understand (or, perhaps more accurately, cannot bear the thought) in these opening scenes that the *inability* to be fully human is itself an aspect of "the lot of all mankind." All mankind is excluded to varying degrees from "eventful experience" and in the desperation and frustration that we share with Faust in our efforts to become more fully human, we each make our own silent (largely unconscious) "deals" with ourselves. These "deals" (which in technical terms might be called "pathological solutions") are not made for the purpose of becoming super-human (which is to become non-human), but for the purpose of becoming more fully human. However, in unconsciously making these "deals" with ourselves, we unwittingly enter more deeply into the non-human—that is, into forms of substitution for life that superficially appear human, but ultimately do not feel either human or alive. For example, as will be discussed in Chapter 3, the perverse individual attempts to bring himself to life by means of compulsively scripted forms of sexual excitement only to find that instead of creating life for himself, he has imprisoned himself in an internal and external object world that is an unchanging imitation (and often a bitter mockery) of living human experience.

Perverse individuals are by no means the only people who enter into unconscious deals with themselves. The unconscious deals we all make with ourselves are psychological events in which we, for example, trade freedom for safety, aliveness for certainty. Of course, the safety and certainty that we secure for ourselves are illusory, but we rely heavily on our illusions. For example, we are, I believe, incapable of both maintaining our sanity and genuinely experiencing our own mortality. Regardless of the enormity of the effort that we might make, we involuntarily avert our gaze at the last moment. In that instant of turning away, we (in fantasy) become immortal and omnipotent and to that degree become less fully alive in the unbearable intensity and immediacy of the present moment.

From this perspective, every form of psychopathology, however extreme or however subtle (and universal), might be thought of as representing a form of unconscious self-limitation of one's capacity to experience being alive as a human being. The limitation of the individual's capacity to be alive may be manifested in a multitude of forms including a constriction of one's range and depth of feeling, thought and bodily sensation, a restriction of one's dream-life and reverie-life, a sense of unrealness in one's relations to oneself and to other people, or a compromise of one's ability to play, to imagine and to use verbal and non-verbal symbols to create/represent one's experience. We not only accept, but embrace these and other limitations of our capacity to be alive when the prospect of being more fully alive as a human being is felt to involve a form of psychic pain that we are afraid we cannot endure. In embracing these forms of psychological deadness, we sacrifice a part of ourselves for the survival of the whole, but find that the "whole" has been sapped of a good deal of vitality in the process.

When I attempt to find words to describe our relationship to ourselves in our efforts to avoid entering into these unconscious "deals" with ourselves, I am reminded of Faulkner's (1946) terse, darkly humorous description of Caddie, the female protagonist of *The Sound and the Fury*: "Doomed and knew it" (p. 10). (Caddie is not even given the benefit of a pronoun in this casually damning verdict that is spit out in four monosyllabic words.) We as analysts are somehow dimly aware of the way in which we are "doomed" (or at least ill-fated) in our strivings to become fully human and in our efforts to assist the analysand in his attempts to do so. Nonetheless, it is in this effort to become more fully human that we are alive as analyst and analysand; it is in this experiment that the art of psychoanalysis lives.

In the chapters that follow, I explore the ways in which the analytic experience is a fabric woven from the warp and the woof of aliveness and deadness, of reverie and interpretation, of privacy and communication, of individuality and intersubjectivity, of the seemingly

ordinary and the deeply personal, of a freedom to
experiment and a groundedness in existing forms, of a
love of imaginative language for itself and the use of
language as a means to a therapeutic end.

2

Analyzing Forms of Aliveness and Deadness

We'll hunt for a third tiger now, but like
The others this one too will be a form
Of what I dream, a structure of words, and not
The flesh and bone tiger that beyond all myths
Paces the earth. I know these things quite well,
Yet nonetheless some force keeps driving me
In this vague, unreasonable, and ancient quest,
And I go on pursuing through the hours
Another tiger, the beast not found in verse.

"The Other Tiger," J.L. Borges, 1960

I have become increasingly aware over the past several years that the sense of aliveness and deadness of the transference-countertransference is, for me, perhaps the single most important measure of the moment-to-moment status of the analytic process. In the course of four clinical discussions, I shall explore the idea that an essential element of analytic technique involves the analyst's making use of his experience in the counter-transference to address specific expressive and defensive roles of the sense of aliveness and deadness of the analysis as well as the particular function of these qualities of experience in the landscape of the patient's internal object world and object relationships. From this perspective, the problems of central concern to analyst and analysand tend to focus increasingly on such questions as: When was the last time the analysis felt alive to both participants? Is there a disguised vitality that cannot be acknowledged by analyst and/or analysand for fear of the consequences of its recognition? What sorts of substitute formations might be masking the lifelessness of the analysis, e.g., manic excitement, perverse pleasure, hysterical acting-in and acting-out, as-if constructions, parasitic dependence on the inner life of the analyst, and so on?

The ideas that I shall present are based in large part on Winnicott's (1971a) conception of the "place where we live" (a third area of experiencing between reality and fantasy [1951]) and the problems involved in generating such a "place" (intersubjective state of mind) in the analysis. I am also drawing heavily upon Bion's (1959) notion that the analyst/mother keeps alive, and in a sense brings to life, the analysand's/infant's projected aspects of self through the successful containment of projective identifications. Symington's (1983) and Coltart's (1986) discussions of the analyst's freedom to think represent important applications to analytic technique of the work of Bion and Winnicott. Green (1983) has made a pivotal contribution to the analytic understanding of the experience of deadness as an early internalization of the unconscious state of the depressed mother.

A great deal has been written in recent years about the importance of the analyst's "realness," i.e., his capacity for spontaneity and freedom to respond to the analysand from his own experience in the analytic situation in a way that is not strangulated by stilted caricatures of analytic neutrality (see for example, Bollas 1987, Casement 1985, Meares 1993, Mitchell 1993, Stewart 1977). As will be clinically illustrated, my own technique rarely includes discussing the countertransference with the patient directly. Instead, the countertransference[1] is implicitly presented in the way I conduct myself as an analyst, for example, in the management of the analytic frame, the tone, wording and content of interpretations and other interventions; in the premium that is placed on symbolization as opposed to tension-dissipating action; and so on.

------

1. I use the term *countertransference* to refer to the analyst's experience of and contribution to the transference-countertransference. The latter term refers to an unconscious intersubjective construction generated by the analytic pair. I do not view transference and countertransference as separable entities that arise in response to one another; rather, I understand these terms to refer to aspects of a single intersubjective totality experienced separately (and individually) by analyst and analysand.

I shall attempt to develop several ideas having to do with technical problems involved in recognizing, symbolizing and interpreting the sense of aliveness and deadness of the analytic experience. I believe that every form of psychopathology represents a specific type of limitation of the individual's capacity to be fully alive as a human being. The goal of analysis from this point of view is larger than that of the resolution of unconscious intrapsychic conflict, the diminution of symptomatology, the enhancement of reflective subjectivity and self-understanding, and the increase of one's sense of personal agency. Although one's sense of being alive is intimately intertwined with each of the above-mentioned capacities, I believe that the experience of aliveness is a quality that is superordinate to these capacities and must be considered as an aspect of the analytic experience *in its own terms*.

The focus of this chapter is clinical. My effort will not be to define psychological aliveness and deadness or even to attempt to describe how we determine whether, or to what extent, a given experience has the quality of aliveness or of deadness. It is not that these questions are unimportant. Rather, the best way I have of addressing these questions is to discuss clinical situations that I believe centrally involve these qualities of experience and to hope that the descriptions themselves convey something of a sense of the ways in which aliveness and deadness are consciously and unconsciously experienced by analyst and analysand. In the four clinical discussions of forms of psychological aliveness and deadness that follow, particular attention is paid to the ways in which countertransference experience is utilized in the process of creating analytic meaning, i.e., in the process of recognizing, symbolizing, understanding, and interpreting the leading transference-countertransference anxiety.

I.

In the first clinical discussion, I will present fragments of an analysis in which the patient's sense of deadness could not initially be symbolized and instead was enacted (entombed) in the lifelessness of the analytic experience itself. The focus of this discussion will be on the use of countertransference to generate verbal symbols that are eventually offered to the patient in the form of interpretations.

Ms. N., a highly successful civic leader, began analysis because she felt intense, but diffuse anxiety and believed that something was seriously wrong in her life, but did not know what it was. In the initial meetings the patient did not seem to consciously experience feelings of emptiness, futility, or stagnation. She said that she felt at a loss for words, which was something that was highly uncharacteristic of her.

The first year-and-a-half of analysis in many ways had the appearance of a satisfactory beginning. The patient was able to see more clearly the specific ways in which she kept people (including me) at a great psychological distance. There was also some decrease in anxiety which was reflected in the patient's increasingly less rigid body posture on the couch. (For almost a year, Ms. N. had lain completely still on the couch with her hands folded on her stomach. At the end of the meeting, the patient would bolt from the couch and briskly leave the room without looking at me.) The language the patient used was initially equally stiff and often sounded textbookish. Her speech pattern became somewhat more natural in the course of the initial year of work. However, the patient throughout this period had profound doubts about whether the analysis was of "any real value" to her. Ms. N. felt that she was developing no greater understanding of either the source of her anxiety or of her sense that things were not right in her life.

In the course of the first half of the second year of work, I gradually developed an awareness of the way in which the patient would fill the hours with apparently introspective talk that did not seem to develop into elements from which further understanding or interpretation could be generated. A pattern developed in the hours in which Ms. N. would describe events in her life in minute detail. It was not at all clear what the point of the lengthy descriptions was. At times, I would say to the patient that I thought that she must be very anxious that I would learn too much about her if she helped me to understand the significance of what she had just said.

I found that I experienced increasingly less curiosity about the patient, which absence had quite a disturbing effect on me. It felt equivalent to losing the use of my mind. I experienced a form of claustrophobia during the hours and on occasion defended against this anxiety by obsessionally counting the minutes until the hour would be over. At other times, I fantasied ending the hour prematurely by telling the patient that I was ill and needed to end the session. I would sometimes "pass the time" by counting the beats per minute of my radial pulse. I was initially unaware that there was anything odd about my taking my pulse despite the fact that this is a practice that has never occurred with any other patient. As the thoughts, feelings, and sensations associated with this activity were occurring, they did not feel like "analytic data." Instead, I experienced them as an almost invisible, private background experience.

During the period of weeks that followed, I gradually became more able to treat the taking of my pulse, as well as the associated feelings and sensations, as "analytic objects" (Bion 1962a, Green 1975, Ogden 1994a, d), i.e., as a reflection of an unconscious construction being generated by the patient and myself, or more accurately being generated by the "intersubjective analytic third." I

analytic
third

have discussed my conception of the "intersubjective analytic third" (or "the analytic third") in a
recent series of publications (Ogden 1992a, b,
1994a, b, c, d). To briefly summarize the ideas presented in those publications, I view the intersubjective analytic third as a third subject created by the
unconscious interplay of analyst and analysand; at
the same time, the analyst and analysand *qua* analyst and analysand are generated in the act of creating the analytic third. (There is no analyst, no
analysand, no analysis, aside from the process
through which the analytic third is generated.)

The new subjectivity (the analytic third)
stands in dialectical tension with the individual
subjectivities of analyst and analysand. I do not
conceive of the intersubjective analytic third as a
static entity; rather, I understand it as an evolving
experience that is continually in a state of flux as
the intersubjectivity of the analytic process is transformed by the understandings generated by the
analytic pair.

The analytic third is experienced through the
individual personality systems of analyst and
analysand and is therefore not an identical experience for each. The creation of the analytic third
reflects the asymmetry of the analytic situation in
that it is created in the context of the analytic setting, which is structured by the relationship of
roles of analyst and analysand. The unconscious
experience of the analysand is privileged in the

analytic relationship; it is the experience of the analysand (past and present) that is taken by the analyst and analysand as the principal (although not exclusive) subject of the analytic dialogue.

I began to be able to link the experience of holding my own wrist (in the act of taking my pulse) with what I now suspected to be a need to literally feel human warmth in an effort to reassure myself that I was alive and healthy. This realization brought with it a profound shift in my understanding of a great many aspects of my experience with Ms. N. I felt moved by the patient's tenacity in telling me seemingly pointless stories for more than 18 months. It occurred to me that these stories had been offered with the unconscious hope that I might find (or create) a point to the stories thereby creating a point (a feeling of coherence, direction, value, and authenticity) for the patient's life. I had previously been conscious of my own fantasy of feigning illness in order to escape the stagnant deadness of the sessions, but I had not understood that this "excuse" reflected an unconscious fantasy that I was being made ill by prolonged exposure to the lifelessness of the analysis. It was through this and similar lines of thought and feeling (associated with my own experience in the analytic third) that I began to develop a sense of the meaning of the patient's diffuse anxiety and her sense that she was caught in something awful that she could not identify. *why did it take him so long?*

I said to Ms. N. that I thought I understood better now some of the reasons for her telling me in great detail about events in her life in a way that made it confusing to both of us why she was telling the story. I said that I felt that she had given up on being able to create a life for herself. Instead, she was giving me the forms with which she had filled her time in hopes that I could create a life for her from these pieces. The patient responded by describing the way in which her life at work and at home consisted almost entirely of organizing other people's activities while never actually making anything herself. It now seemed to her that she used other people's lives and the things that they made (the lives of her employees, of her husband, her au pair, and her two children) as substitutes for her own ability to create something that felt like a life of her own.

Later in the session, she said that she had for a long time imagined that a paperweight on a table next to my chair had been a gift from a patient. She said that she had never told me that she had even noticed the object, but that she had for a long time wished that she had given it to me. It was not until that moment that she realized that she had not imagined giving me a gift of her own, and instead had wished that she had given me *that gift*. She could not envision herself as a person who could select, and in that sense create, a gift for me, so she imagined being someone else, the person who had given me the gift. I thought, but did not interpret at this juncture, that underlying this thought was the fantasy that it would never be possible for her to create a life of her own so the only alternative available to her was that of stealing the life of another person. It seemed important that I not usurp the patient's opportunity to create life in the analysis (create interpretations) that she was now just beginning to be able to do.

Several months later, Ms. N. presented a dream in which she was in a cabinet in a kitchen that was not her own kitchen. It was as if she had been "poured into the cabinet" and had become a rectangular cube the shape of the inside of the wooden box. The dream was presented in conjunction with the patient's telling me about a friend who lived with continual psychological pain in connection with the death of her five-year-old daughter. The friend's child had been killed before the patient began analysis in an accident that had resulted from the negligence of a babysitter.

After telling me the dream, Ms. N. fell silent. This silence stood in marked contrast to the way in which she had in the past obscured feeling with excessive verbiage. After a few minutes, I said to Ms. N. that I thought that she was describing to me her sense that she lacked a shape of her own. I went on to say that her friend's pain, however terrible, was a human feeling that I thought the patient feared she was incapable of experiencing. I told her that although she had never said so directly, I felt that she was afraid that she might never be able to feel anything, even the pain that others might feel about the death of their child.

In a voice so faint that I could barely hear her, Ms. N. said that this had for a long time been a fear of hers about which she felt profound shame. She had stayed awake many nights worrying that she would be unable to grieve if one of her own children were to die and that this felt to her to be the most odious failure of which any mother could be guilty. She said that she felt that she had not been able to love and be with her children in the way she wished she could have been. In fact, she now knew that she had neglected them quite badly and that they had suffered greatly for it. The patient again fell silent for the remaining few minutes of the hour.

To summarize, I view the portion of the analysis just discussed as representing the beginnings of a process in which the patient's experience of deadness (both in her imagined inability to grieve and in her identification with her friend's dead child) was being transformed from an unthinkable thing-in-itself (a fact experienced by both the patient and myself as a non-verbally symbolized sense of deadness of the analysis) into a living, verbally symbolized experience of the patient's (and my own) deadness in the analysis. An intersubjective analytic space had begun to be generated in which the deadness could be felt, viewed, experienced, and spoken about by the two of us. Deadness had become a feeling as opposed to a fact.

II.

In this second clinical discussion, I shall describe an analytic encounter which illustrates technical challenges arising in conjunction with a patient's unconscious insistence that the analyst serve as the repository for his psychic life and hope.

Mr. D., in the initial interview, informed me that he had been in analysis six times and each time "had been terminated" by the analyst. The most recent unilateral termination had occurred three months prior to Mr. D.'s first meeting with me.

The patient carried himself and spoke in a way that conveyed a sense of arrogance, aloofness, and self-importance; at the same time, this deportment had a brittleness to it that made it readily apparent that the patient's superior tone of voice and demeanor thinly disguised feelings of fear, worthlessness, and desperation.

Mr. D. told me that if he were to continue past our initial meeting, I must understand that he would never be the one who spoke first in any session. He explained that if I were to attempt to "wait him out," the session would be spent in complete silence. He had wasted his time and money in that way too many times in the past and hoped that I would not repeat that approach with him. He added that it would also be a waste of time for me to ask him about the "fears and anxieties" underlying his inability to begin the session: "After all, my answering questions of that sort would be tantamount to my beginning the hour—you know that as well as I do."

Mr. D.'s presentation of himself intrigued me and stirred feelings of competitiveness in me. He had thrown down the gauntlet and I would prove myself to be more adept and agile than the previous six analysts. In the initial interview I was also aware that I was unconsciously being invited to take the role of a suitor and that there was a fantasied homosexual sadomasochistic scene that was already beginning to take shape in the trans-ference-countertransference. At the same time, I recognized that the fantasy of entering into a competitive game protected me from fully feeling the deadly seriousness of the intense contempt and hatred that I was encountering. In addition, the narcissistic/competitive fantasy protected me from feelings of being trapped in the web that Mr. D. was already beginning to spin with his imperiously controlling instructions regarding the way in which the analysis was to be con-ducted. I imagined that long years of isolation awaited both of us if we were to undertake analy-sis together.

I said to Mr. D. that I thought he imagined that analysis with me would involve one or both of us brutalizing the other until the one being brutalized could no longer bear it. I also said that I had no interest in brutalizing him, being brutalized by him or participating in his brutalization of himself. This comment was not meant as a reassurance, but as a statement about my conception of the analytic framework within which I was willing to work. I agreed to be the first to speak in each hour, but said that I would do so only when I thought I had something to say. I added that it might sometimes take me a good deal of time to be able to put my experience into words for myself and for him at the beginning of the session, but my silence would not be intended as an attempt to "wait him out."

Mr. D. sat quietly and seemed to relax a bit as I spoke. I was somewhat encouraged by the fact that I felt that I had been able to say something to him that did not involve a sadistic attack on Mr. D. nor a compromise of either of us. Neither did it seem to me to involve a form of manic excitement and denial related to the fantasy of a competitive game.

At the outset of each of the meetings with Mr. D., I attempted to find words to convey what it felt like being with him in that particular moment. I (silently) hypothesized that both the fantasies and feelings about brutalization and the fantasies reflecting manic excitement (competition) in the transference-countertransference represented forms of defense against the experience of inner deadness, which deadness was symbolized by Mr. D.'s feeling that he had nothing in him with which to begin the hours (to begin his story). I would have to be the one to bring life to the analysis (to create history) each time we met. Almost always as I began the hour, I had the conscious fantasy that I was giving the patient and the analysis mouth-to-mouth resuscitation. I chose not to tell Mr. D. about this fantasy directly in order not to demean him nor to prematurely address the homosexual aspects of the transference-countertransference.

At times, what I said to Mr. D. to begin the hour felt rote and hackneyed and I labored to get beyond what felt like pre-fabricated analytic cliché in order not to dump further lifelessness into him and into the analysis. In one of these meetings very early on in the analysis I told Mr. D. that I found myself imagining attempting to lure him into trusting me. I said that I knew that this would not only be futile, but would also be destructive since anything "won" by me in this way would be experienced by both of us as a form of theft that would alienate us from one another even further than we already were. After several minutes of silence, Mr. D. described his continual vigilance in combating theft: his use of burglar alarms at his home, anti-theft devices in his car, a safe at his office, and so on. This was spoken in a way that gave no acknowledgment that it represented a response to what I

had just said. Despite the patient's offering information of this sort, the feeling in the hour was that
of an extremely tense stand-off which threatened
to break apart at any moment. It felt as if there
were nothing human holding the fabric of the
analysis together.

In a session that occurred in the sixth month
of the analysis, I thought for a moment that I saw
tears brimming in Mr. D.'s eyes, but when I looked
more closely I could not tell if my perception had
been accurate. (Mr. D. was at that point refusing to
use the couch and so we were meeting face to
face.) I told Mr. D. what had just occurred and said
that whether or not there had been tears in his
eyes, I felt that what had happened reflected the
sadness of the situation that he and I were in. (I
remembered Mr. D.'s telling me some months earlier that he had been grateful to his previous analyst for her honesty in telling him that she could
not be of help to him instead of mindlessly persist-
ing in an analysis that she felt could not progress.
That thought reminded me of a "living will" that
had recently been sent to me by a member of my
family in which doctors were in effect instructed
not to create an empty illusion of life after genuine
life had already been lost.)

Mr. D. sat quietly for a minute and said that
he had not been moved by my "little speech." He
then returned to his silence. After about five minutes, I said I thought that what had just happened

between us must reflect something basic to his experience. I had felt sadness, part of which was no doubt my own, something attributable to my own sense of extreme loneliness in being with him. I added that nonetheless I felt that in part I was feeling something for him, in his stead. I said that I had in the past tried to talk with him about it, but that his replies had always made me feel as if I were either crazy or stupid or both. I said that if I were not in a position to feel some confidence in my ability to differentiate between what feels real and what does not, I would find it a great strain to have my perceptions drawn into question in such a fundamental way. I told him that it would surprise me greatly if at important points in his life, he had not felt this type of strain in relation to his own ability to differentiate which parts of his experience and perceptions were real and which were not. It seemed from my experience in being with him that he must have felt powerfully assaulted in his efforts to hold onto a conviction about the truth of what he thought, saw, felt, heard, and so on.

The patient seemed to ignore almost all of what I had just said and instead commented that I had used the word "brutalized" in our first meeting. That word was the most accurate word, and "maybe the only accurate word," that I had used in all these months of analysis. He said that he had never been beaten or abused as a child, but he had felt that he had been brutalized in subtle and in not so subtle ways that he cannot describe because he is not even sure what occurred, if in fact anything out of the ordinary did occur. Mr. D. said that he would not try to tell me about his childhood because it was all very normal—"I've gone over it a hundred times with my previous analysts and there isn't anything that would earn me a place on the Donahue Show."

This exchange was the closest Mr. D. and I had come to talking to one another. Over the next several weeks, he became increasingly antagonistic and disparaging of me and the analysis. I interpreted the fact that his attacks on me and our efforts to talk to one another had increased dramatically after the meeting that I have just described. At one point, the patient expressed great contempt for my use of the word "work" to describe what was occurring in these "very expensive hours." I said to Mr. D. that earlier he had commented on my use of another word, the word "brutalized." I told him that I thought that his having acknowledged feeling understood by me, if only in my use of that single word, had led him to feel that things between the two of us had become wildly and dangerously out of control. I said that I thought that what currently appeared on the surface to be his brutalizing me felt to me more like an effort to protect me by getting me to throw him out. I added that I suspected that if I did not soon terminate our meetings he would end the analysis

as the only way he felt he had at his disposal to protect me from what he feared to be his endlessly
escalating brutalization of me. Mr. D. did not end
the analysis, but for a period of almost six months
he turned his chair at the beginning of the meeting so that his back was to me. I suspect that he did
not want me to be able to see his eyes. In that
phase of work, he spoke even less than in the initial months of analysis.

In the portion of the analysis discussed above, Mr.
D. had in fantasy put into me the fragile remainder of
his sense of life and hope. I was to speak for him and
feel for him (by beginning each meeting and by being
the container of his projective identifications involving
his profound loneliness and sadness) while he attacked
me for being so naïve as to imagine that I could safe-
guard his life and my own in the face of his immense
brutality. Extreme splitting of the brutalized and brutalizing aspects of the patient had been a necessary condition for any form of relatedness to me to be
sustained. In the course of the analysis, the patient
began to experience for himself the rudiments of sadness and compassion for the aspects of himself which
he had projected into me and had experienced
through me.

III.

In ongoing consultation with clinicians who come to me to discuss analyses that they are conducting, I ask that the analyst attempt to talk with me not only about what the analysis and analysand say to one another, but also about the analyst's moment-to-moment thoughts, feelings, and sensations. The analyst is asked to include this aspect of his work in his process notes that he records during the analytic hours and discusses with me in our consultation meetings. In addition, I suggest that the analyst write process notes for all meetings including those that the patient fails to attend. I operate under the assumption that the patient's physical absence creates a specific form of psychological effect in the analyst and in the analysis and that the analytic process continues despite the analysand's physical absence. In this way, the specific meanings of the patient's presence in his absence are transformed into analytic objects to be fully experienced, lived with, symbolized, understood, and made part of the analytic discourse.

In using process notes in this way, the analyst attempts to symbolize and speak to himself about his experience with the patient no matter how seemingly unrelated to the analysand, the analyst's fantasies, physical sensations, ruminations, daydreams, and so on might appear to be (Ogden 1992a, b, 1994a, b, c, d). I do not "insist" that a supervisee discuss with me this aspect of the analytic experience since some analysts are initially temperamentally incapable of attending to this level of their experience. Moreover, the analysts consulting with me are not always sufficiently at ease with themselves or with me to entrust this aspect of their work to me. However, I have found that as the supervisory relationship unfolds, supervisees are usually able to develop these capabilities and make use of this aspect of the analytic experience in their therapeutic work and in consultation. I have also found that it is rare for a therapist to be able to engage in this form of supervisory experience without having previously taken part in a successful personal analysis. In the absence of such an experience in analysis (which is not to invoke the illusion of the "completed analysis"), it is unusual for a therapist to have developed the capacity to make analytic use of his mundane, quotidian, unobtrusive thoughts, feelings, and sensations that occupy him during the analytic hours.

As with most aspects of analytic technique, attention to and use of the analyst's private discourse that is seemingly unrelated to the patient runs counter to the character defenses that we have developed in the course of our lives. To attempt to loosen our dependence on these character defenses often feels like "tearing off a layer of skin," leaving us with a diminished stimulus barrier with which to protect the boundary between inner and outer, between receptivity and overstimulation, between sanity and insanity.

The analytic work that I shall now describe occurred in the context of the supervision of an analyst

who had been consulting with me on a weekly basis for
about a year. The analysis had begun in a way that was
quite disappointing to the analyst.

> The analysand, Dr. C., was a resident in family
> practice medicine who had read about psychoanal-
> ysis in college, medical school, and residency. He
> had a strong sense of the "rules of analysis" and
> complied with them, although from the beginning
> he complained about the rigidity of the "game,"
> for example, the analysand's having to pay for
> missed meetings, the "requirement" that the
> analysand take his vacations when the analyst does,
> the demand for compliance with the "fundamen-
> tal rule," and so on. (With the exception of the fee
> arrangement, the analyst had said nothing about
> these "rules.")
>
> Dr. C.'s reasons for being in analysis were
> vague: he felt he should "learn about himself" as
> part of his training as a family practice physician.
> The idea that he was asking for help with the psy-
> chological pain that he was experiencing would
> have represented an imagined act of submission
> that the patient could not have tolerated at the
> beginning of the analysis. The analysand was on
> time for each session and compliantly "free associ-
> ated," presenting a blend of dreams, childhood
> memories, sexual fantasies, and current work-
> related, marital and child-rearing difficulties and
> stresses. There were confessions of secret acts

about which the patient felt shame, for example, the use of pornographic magazines during masturbation and two incidents of cheating on medical school laboratory reports.

However, from the earliest days and weeks of analysis, the analyst, Dr. F., experienced the patient as boring to a degree to which he was unaccustomed. It felt as if the patient were attempting to imitate what he had imagined went on in a "good analysis." It required considerable forbearance for Dr. F. to refrain from entering into the analysis with interpretations of the content that was being presented, for example, interpretation of dream material that "seemed to beg for transference interpretations." In consultation, Dr. F. discussed the possible interpretations that he might have made, but had chosen to defer. It seemed to me that these interpretations would have been imitations of "deep" transference interpretations and would have been offered in an effort on the part of Dr. F. to create his own fantasy of a "good analysis." As time went on, the analyst felt greatly tempted to chastise the analysand or even comment contemptuously on the emptiness of the patient's verbiage. At each stage, an important perspective that was elaborated in the consultation included the idea that it was of critical importance for Dr. F. not to enter into an empty (inert) discourse with the patient and at the same time it was crucial that the analyst maintain his capacity to entertain any thought, feeling, or sensation that arose within him (see Bion 1978, Symington 1983). No possible interpretation or response to the patient was to be reflexively dismissed or stifled. It required enormous psychological effort on the part of Dr. F. to resist becoming mechanical, detached, or imitative of an idealized version of his own analyst or of me.

Dr. F. developed his own style of taking process notes in which he was able to capture something of the totality of the experience of the hour including the details of his own experience. I think of this as the effort of the analyst to focus upon the countertransference aspects of the transference-countertransference as "total situation" (Joseph 1985, Klein 1952, Ogden 1991a). In other words, it is the transference-countertransference, not simply the transference, that constitutes the matrix in which psychological meanings are generated in the analytic situation.

As Dr. F. would present the hours to me in our weekly consultation sessions, neither of us felt pressured to draw one-to-one correspondences between Dr. F.'s thoughts and feelings and those of the patient. At times, we each offered tentative understandings of the relationship between Dr. F.'s experience and what was happening in the analytic hour. Usually, Dr. F.'s reveries were simply noted and were allowed to reverberate within him and within me as we listened to the subsequent material. We sometimes referred back in our discussions to reveries that Dr. F. had presented in consultation meetings weeks or months earlier.

Dr. F.'s thoughts in the initial months of analysis often included wishful images of his upcoming vacations or of memories of recent browsing in interesting shops and bookstores during his afternoon breaks. These were understood not simply as generic escapist fantasies, but in each instance were felt to reflect a specific response to what was occurring in the analysis at that particular moment. At one point, several of Dr. F.'s vacation daydreams were of an unrealistically idealized sort and seemed to reflect the make-believe nature of the analysis. The patient did not want an actual analysis, he defensively desired a perfect one. In other words, the analysand unconsciously wished for an omnipotently created analysis that did not involve actual encounters between himself and another person with all the anxieties associated with the human lapses, misunderstandings, and so on that that would have entailed.

Dr. F. attempted to keep alive in himself his capacity to be curious, to question, to comment spontaneously on what was occurring in the analytic interaction despite the "canned" responses that he would often receive from the patient. "Analytic etiquette" was not treated as sacred by Dr. F. much to the surprise and disapproval of the patient. For instance, the patient at one point indicated that he wanted advice from Dr. F., but immediately added that he knew that Dr. F. could not give him advice. Dr. F. responded by asking the patient why he could not give the patient advice. In the end, no advice was given, and instead there was a discussion of the patient's use of fantasied rules (his own omnipotent creations and projections) for the purpose of preventing himself from experiencing and thinking about the personal, idiosyncratic, unpredictable nature of the experience that was occurring between Dr. F. and himself.

When Dr. F. found himself feeling curious about an aspect of the material that the patient was discussing, he asked the patient for further details even when the questions seemed tangential. For example, at one point, Dr. F. asked the patient for the name of a restaurant that the patient had parenthetically mentioned having enjoyed the previous evening. The analyst was well aware that the omission of the detail (the name of the restaurant) very likely represented a way of tantalizing and excluding the analyst (a projection of the patient's curiosity and feeling of exclusion from the life of the analyst). However, at the time, Dr. F. decided to ask (perhaps more accurately, found himself asking) for the detail about which he felt curious while deferring exploration of the tantalizing effect of the omission of this particular detail. (Coltart [1986] has made a similar recommendation with regard to allowing oneself to laugh at a patient's jokes before analyzing the conscious and unconscious motivations of the patient's wish to get the analyst to laugh.)

It should be emphasized that while Dr. F. attempted to insure space in the analysis for spontaneity and "freedom of thought," he by no means treated the analytic frame in a cavalier manner— hours were begun and ended in a timely way; casual conversation did not occur between the waiting room and the consulting room; suggestion, reassurance, exhortation, and the like played no larger a part in this analysis than in others conducted by this careful and thoughtful analyst.

For most of the first year of analysis, Dr. F. felt that the life of the analysis resided almost entirely in his own capacity to maintain his freedom for reverie during the analytic hours and in his discussions with me of these reveries. By the beginning of the first half of the second year of analysis, the patient began to evidence changes in his ability to speak with a voice of his own that no longer seemed quite as clichéd, stereotypic, and imitative as before. However, the changes seemed fragile and short-lived to Dr. F.

In this period of analysis, Dr. F. presented a session in consultation in which the patient was silent for the first few minutes of the meeting. Dr. F. told me that during this period of silence he had been thinking about the fact that I would be spending my Christmas break in Hawaii. He wondered if I would bring Christmas presents along with me on the trip, all wrapped in shiny red and green paper. He imagined how odd it would be to exchange Christmas gifts in Hawaii and pictured my wife giving me a woolen sweater as a Christmas gift. I commented that I thought Dr. F. was expressing skepticism about some of the ideas that we had been discussing in the course of the supervision, particularly the emphasis I had been placing on the importance of Dr. F.'s capacity for creativity and spontaneity in his work (as opposed to adopting reflexive, imitative, pre-fabricated approaches).

In the course of discussing Dr. F.'s reverie concerning my vacation, I said to Dr. F. that I thought that he was depicting me as participating in a self-deceptive charade in which I was treating Christmas as something that could be dug up and moved from one place to another without any change in the experience as one might move a plant from one side of a garden to another. The feeling in the daydream was that Christmas had become entirely a form for me and that I had lost touch with any meaning or feeling beyond the conventional activities associated with it. This reverie depicted Dr. F.'s disappointment, as well as some degree of competitive pleasure, in viewing me as lacking self-understanding with regard to my own mechanicalness.

It seemed to both Dr. F. and to me that Dr. F. was saying to both of us, "Ogden talks a good game

about realness, authenticity, genuineness, spontaneity, and so on, but when it comes down to it,
maybe he doesn't know what's real and what isn't."
Dr. F. and I discussed the way in which my placing
a premium on spontaneity may have created a
dilemma of sorts for Dr. F.: he may have begun to
find himself attempting to "train himself" to be
spontaneous. To make matters worse, he may have
unconsciously felt that "achieving spontaneity"
would involve imitating me. Dr. F. came to see
more clearly as a result of the discussion of this
Christmas reverie that his patient had been labor-
ing under a similar burden in the analysis for some
time. For months, Dr. C. had said that he felt an
internal pressure to be "on" in analysis, that is, to
be interesting to Dr. F. Only at this point did Dr.
C.'s comment take on an analytic meaning
(become an "analytic object") that could be symbolized, reflected upon, and interpreted. Dr. F.
felt that he now better understood that the
patient's internal pressure to be "on" reflected the
patient's unconscious fantasy that he could only be
alive for Dr. F. to the degree that he could learn to
think, feel, speak, and behave in a manner like or
the same as Dr. F. This placed the patient in an
impossible position in which feeling alive and
being interesting to Dr. F. had become synony-
mous. Paradoxically, the idea of feeling alive had
for Dr. C. become unconsciously equivalent to
becoming (an idealized version of) Dr. F.

In the course of the succeeding weeks of analysis, Dr. F. offered to the analysand his understanding of this dilemma that he believed to underlie Dr. C.'s feeling of pressure to be "on" in analysis. Both this interpretation and Dr. F.'s self-understanding upon which it rested facilitated the creation of psychological space in the analysis in which both the patient and the analyst were able to continue to develop their capacity to generate thoughts, feelings and sensations without feeling that there was an unstated script or paradigm that either of them was being asked to mouth or imitate.

In the clinical sequence just described, it was essential for the analyst to be able to have his own thoughts independent of mine (which need was symbolized by Dr. F.'s unconscious criticism of me in the Christmas reverie). Only when Dr. F. became aware of the way in which his own capacity for original thought had been paralyzed by his fear of confronting his defensive idealization of me, could he regain his full capacity for reverie. Dr. F.'s symbolization of, and understanding of, this defensive process as it was portrayed in the Christmas reverie formed the basis for his interpretation of his patient's futile attempts to overcome his own experience of deadness by (in fantasy) attempting to become a perfect patient, that is, to become a defensively idealized version of his conception of an analytic patient.

IV.

The final clinical vignette that I shall present will focus
on the problem of "competing" (Tustin 1980, see also
Ogden 1989a, b) with a form of deadness that involves
a pathologically autistic aspect of personality. In the
analysis of adult patients, the autistic component of the
personality is often not at all evident in the beginning
of analysis (S. Klein 1980). This was the case in the
analysis of Mrs. S.

In the initial analytic meeting, Mrs. S. talked about
her difficulties in "getting her life together." She
had not been able to graduate from college as a
result of her inability to concentrate. Her marriage
was in disarray and she felt on the edge of panic.

It is not possible in the space of the present
paper to offer an account of the stages of the evolution of the analytic process over the first eight
years of this five session per week analysis. The outcome of these years of work might very broadly be
summarized by saying that despite the fact that
there had been important changes in the patient's
ability to function in the world (for example, she
was able to graduate from college and hold a
responsible job), the patient's capacity to enter
into relationships with other people remained very
limited. Mrs. S. and her husband slept in separate
bedrooms and on occasion engaged in what the
patient described as "mechanical sex." It had

required more than five years of analysis for the patient to even recognize that she "managed" her three children as if she were "an employee of a daycare center" and that she had very little sense of each of them as individuals. Her friendships were shallow and only toward the end of the seventh year of analysis did she begin to feel the absence of loving relationships in her life.

In the analytic relationship, I was again and again stunned (in a way that I have rarely experienced with other patients) by the depth of the patient's inability to evidence or experience any warmth toward me. It was not that Mrs. S. did not feel dependent on me. She was greatly distressed by weekend breaks, vacations (her own as well as mine), the end of each session, and would frequently telephone my answering machine in order to hear my voice (without leaving a message of her own). However, Mrs. S. experienced her dependence not as a personal attachment, but as an addiction that she deeply resented. She once instructed me, "A heroin addict does not love heroin. The fact that she'll kill to get it doesn't mean she loves it or feels any kind of affection for it." The patient felt powerfully untouchable in her isolation and seemed to value this feeling of "being immune to human vulnerabilities" more than anything else in life. This "untouchable" quality was reflected in her anorectic symptomatology. The patient subsisted on a diet of fruit, grains and vegetables and organized her life around a rigorous exercise regime that included marathon jogging and the extensive use of a stationary bicycle. The patient exercised vigorously for at least three hours every day. If the exercise routine were in any way disrupted (for example, by illness or by travel), the patient would experience a state of intense anxiety that on two occasions developed into a full blown panic attack. Mrs. S., at the beginning of the analysis, experienced no appetite for food, sex, ideas, art, or anything else. The patient's weight held the greatest importance for her: by maintaining a particular weight (at the very low end of what she could tolerate physiologically without falling physically ill), she experienced a form of power that allowed her in fantasy to control everything that might occur both within her and outside of her.

It would be inaccurate to say that the patient always felt numb or without feelings in the analytic hours. Mrs. S. frequently experienced intense anger, which she called "hatred," toward me. However, her anger never seemed personal. By this I mean that it never felt as if her anger had anything to do with me. The hatred did not even seem to be the patient's personal creation; rather, it seemed like a blind, reflexive almost convulsive thrashing about that occurred when her sense of absolute control and ownership of me was compromised. Since I was the person/object who happened to be there, it was I who happened to be the object of her rage. Mrs. S.'s criticism of me always involved her projective fantasy of my omnipotence: she felt that I could easily give her what she needed if I chose to, but I stubbornly refused to do so.

Other than her single-minded crusade to gain access to my fantasied omnipotent power there seemed to be very little about me that was of interest to the patient. It was difficult for me to accept how little I seemed to mean to this patient outside of the terms of the fantasy I am discussing. For years, I held to the belief that Mrs. S. secretly loved me (albeit in a primitive way), felt a form of concern for me, knew something about who I am as a person, but stubbornly refused to admit it. This belief was based on the intensity of the patient's feeling of dependence on me in conjunction with the fact that I felt concern for and interest in her. At times, I interpreted what I felt to be the patient's anxiety about acknowledging any feeling of human connection with me for fear of the loss of control over her external and internal world that that would entail. She would respond by saying that what I said might be true, but she was not aware of feeling affection, love, warmth or even concern for me or for anyone else for that matter. The defensive function of such a stance on the patient's part was discussed on many occasions, but did not lead to any discernible affective change. (These interpretations felt increasingly stale to both the patient and to me.)

Perhaps it was the patient's response to the death of my father that was the beginning of my loosening of my hold on the belief that the patient secretly felt some form of love or concern for me. The events transpiring between Mrs. S. and myself around this event (in the eighth year of analysis) led me to feel that there was a qualitative difference between the human disconnectedness achieved by Mrs. S. and forms of defense against the dangers of love and hate that I had encountered with other patients. After receiving the unexpected news of my father's death, I telephoned my patients and supervisees to tell them that there had been a death in my family and that I would be canceling several days' meetings. I told each of them that I would phone them to tell them when I would be resuming work. When I spoke with Mrs. S., she received the news quietly, but immediately asked me if I knew approximately when I would be returning to work. I said that I did not know, but would let her know when I did.

In our first meeting after my return, Mrs. S. said that she was "sorry that someone in my family had died." There was unmistakable anger in her voice as she underscored the vagueness of the word "someone." She fell silent for a few minutes and then said that it made her feel furious not to know who it was who had died and said that she felt that I had been sadistic in not giving her that information when I phoned her. She added that she was certain that I had told all my other patients who it was in my family that had died. During this interchange, I felt deeply disturbed by a recognition against which I had struggled for most of a decade: it seemed to me that Mrs. S. was unable to feel anything for me as a human being beyond her need to protect herself by means of her efforts to magically enter me and control me from within.

At this point in the meeting, I began to recall the details of the feelings that I had felt during the telephone call that I had made to Mrs. S. soon after I learned of my father's death. I remembered with great vividness the feeling of attempting to control my voice as I spoke to her in an effort to hold back tears. I wondered whether it was possible that she had heard nothing of that. How could she have not experienced that moment (as I had) as one in which there had been a close connection between the two of us? Instead, she apparently experienced it as still another occasion in which her omnipotent wishes had been frustrated.

I could hear the voice with which I was speaking to myself at that moment in the meeting as the voice of a person experiencing a sense of inpenetrable alienation from Mrs. S.; at the same time, I also recognized something else in that voice for the first time. It was the voice of a spurned lover. It occurred to me that Mrs. S. lived in a world in which two different forms of human experience each disguised the other.

At that juncture, I felt that I had arrived at the beginnings of an understanding of something about the relationship between Mrs. S. and myself that I had not previously grasped. This new understanding did not serve to protect me from the chilling inhumanness that I had sensed in Mrs. S. and which I knew reflected important autistic and paranoid-schizoid elements in her personality; neither did it serve to dim the recognition that alongside these powerful autistic and paranoid-schizoid defenses was a capacity for human love. I could at this point see in retrospect that it was in part my own lack of compassion for Mrs. S. and her wishes to comfort me *as my wife* that had led me to blind myself to the fact that her seeming absence of compassion represented a complex interplay of two powerful, coexisting aspects of her personality. She had been concerned about me and felt despondent that her love was unrecognizable to me (for example, as reflected in my not allowing her to comfort me). At the same time there was an important way in which Mrs. S. was unable to come to life as a human being and instead occupied a mechanical, omnipotent world of (1) relatedness to "autistic shapes" and "autistic objects" (Tustin 1980, 1984) (for example, the mechanical, self-sufficiency involved in the sensation-world of exercise and diet) and, (2) paranoid-schizoid fantasies of entering me and parasitically living in me and through me.

I had been unable to live with, formulate, and interpret for myself and for the patient the mutually obscuring interrelationship between being alive and being dead (i.e., the coexistence of depressive, paranoid-schizoid and autistic-contiguous [Ogden 1989a, b] dimensions of the patient's personality). Mrs. S. had loved me and had felt nothing whatsoever for me at the same time. I had experienced affection for her (which I came to recognize more fully in my experience of feeling like a spurned lover), but could not allow myself to feel warmth or at times even feel compassion for someone who was so clearly inhuman and inhumane (for example, in her treatment of her husband, her children and in her response to me, particularly after my father's death).

Later in the session that I am describing, I said to Mrs. S. that I thought I had underestimated two things in our relationship: the amount of affection that there was and the degree to which no relationship at all existed between us. When I lost sight of one or the other facet of the situation, I failed to understand the totality of who she is and who we are together. I added that I thought that the degree to which it was possible for there to be no human tie between us had diminished in the time that we had known one another, but that it remained a considerable force to be reckoned with.

Mrs. S. responded by saying that I had never spoken to her in that way before. Previously, she had always felt that there was a way in which I was as cold as she was and that she could hear the iciness in my voice. She could not detect that coldness in me just now. Mrs. S. went on to say that she did not believe that that iciness was gone, but at least it did not dominate everything that occurred between us for the moment.

I understood this to be a statement of the patient's feeling of relief in her sense that she could accept understanding from me, which was something she never before had been able to do without immediately attacking it, or more often, withdrawing into a state of autistic self-sufficiency or omnipotent paranoid-schizoid defensive fantasy. My interpretation had denied neither her emotional deadness (her paranoid-schizoid and autistic-contiguous modes of protecting herself) nor her increased capacity to experience a human connection to me (albeit very sparingly acknowledged by her).

Concluding Comments

I have presented four clinical discussions in an effort to illustrate ways in which the sense of aliveness and deadness are generated and experienced in and through the intersubjective analytic third. In each of the clinical situations described, the analyst attempted to create analytic meaning ("analytic objects") from that which had been unconsciously present in, and powerfully shaping of, the analytic encounter, but had been fore-closed from the analytic discourse. It was through the analyst's use of his reveries, his unobtrusive, quotidian, thoughts, feelings, and sensations (often seemingly unrelated to the patient) that specific, verbally symbol-ized meanings were generated and eventually utilized in the interpretive process. In the four analyses described, the particular quality of the experience of aliveness and deadness generated in the transference-countertransference constituted an important intersub-jective construction that reflected a central aspect of the analysand's pathologically structured internal object world.

— 3 —

The Perverse Subject of Analysis

It is by now widely accepted that the analysis of perversion is not fundamentally a process of decoding and interpreting the unconscious fantasies, anxieties, and defenses that are enacted in the perverse patient's sexual activity. Instead, it has become increasingly recognized that the analysis of perversion centrally involves the understanding and interpretation of transference phenomena that are structured by the patient's perverse internal object world (Malcolm 1970, Meltzer 1973). I believe it is important that this evolving understanding be developed a step further: in my view, the analysis of perversion necessarily involves the analysis of the *perverse transference-countertransference* as it unfolds in the analytic relationship.

In analyzing perversion, one cannot hope to understand what the patient is attempting to communicate without (to some extent) entering into the perverse scene that is being created in the transference-countertransference. As a result, an analyst attempting to write about the analysis of perversion must describe something of his own experience in (of) the perverse transference-countertransference; otherwise, he must content himself with presenting a desiccated, detached, and ultimately false picture of the analysis that fails to capture the experience of the Siren song of the perverse scene in which he has unwittingly participated.[1]

In this chapter, I will illustrate, through a detailed clinical discussion, the way in which a form of perversity of the transference-countertransference derives from a core experience of psychological deadness. The story of this form of perversion is the fantasied history of the stillbirth of the self resulting from an unconsciously fantasied empty parental intercourse. It is a story that cannot be told (i.e., experienced by the subject) since the subject (a stillborn infant) is dead and therefore

---

1. The perverse intersubjective constructions generated in the course of the analysis of perversion are, in my experience, inevitably (to a considerable degree) inaccessible to the analyst's conscious awareness as they are unfolding. It is therefore necessary for the analyst to attempt ". . . to catch the drift of the patient's unconscious with his own unconscious" (Freud 1923a, p. 239). The analyst must in a sense come to understand the perverse transference-countertransference "after the fact," i.e., in the course of his doing the psychological work required to become aware of his own *unconscious* experience of (and participation in) the perverse transference-countertransference.

the very act of telling (creating) a story is a lie, a charade. Paradoxically, the lie and the recognition of its falsehood in the context of an analytic discourse is the only real locus of truth (the only experience that feels real to both analyst and analysand).

The type of perverse process that will be discussed is understood as centrally involving the subversion of the recognition of the psychological death of the subject (and of the emptiness of the analytic discourse in which he or she is engaged), and the replacement of this recognition with an illusory subject, the perverse subject of analysis. The perverse subject of analysis is the narrator of the erotized, but ultimately empty drama created on the analytic stage. The drama itself is designed to present the false impression that the narrator (the perverse subject) is alive in his or her power to excite. The perverse analytic scene and the perverse subject of analysis are jointly constructed by analyst and analysand for the purpose of evading the experience of psychological deadness and the recognition of the emptiness of the analytic discourse/intercourse. In a sense, the perverse subject of analysis constitutes a third analytic subject intersubjectively created by, and experienced through, the individual subjectivities of analyst and analysand in the context of their separate, but interrelated personality systems. Consequently, the jointly created intersubjective construction (the perverse subject) is experienced differently by analyst and analysand. (In a recent series of publications [Ogden 1992a, b, 1994a, b, c, d], I have discussed the concept of the intersubjective analytic third as well as specific forms of the intersubjective third such as the subjugating third of projective identification [Ogden 1994c,d].)

Perversion of the transference-countertransference occurs in all analyses to different degrees. For some patients, it is the dominant form of analytic interaction, eclipsing all other modes of defense and object relatedness. For other patients, it is in ascendancy only in a specific phase or phases of analysis. For still other patients, perversity in (of) the transference-countertransference represents a background that presents itself primarily in the form of a well disguised sexual excitement associated with unconscious efforts on the part of the patient to thwart the analysis in fundamental, but difficult to recognize ways (for example, the patient's unconscious excitement associated with his or her chronic inability/unwillingness to generate a single, original thought in the analysis [Ogden, 1994b]).

The understandings of perversion that will be discussed here rely heavily on ideas introduced by several analytic thinkers practicing in England and France. Khan (1979) has illuminated the way in which perversity represents a compulsively repeated effort to create experience that will disguise and partially substitute for the absence of a sense of being alive as a human being. McDougall (1978, 1986) has discussed the need of the sexually deviant patient to generate "neo-sexualities" in an effort to construct a self, albeit a self and a sexuality that is felt to be fragmentary, defensive, and unreal. Chasseguet-Smirgel (1984) has described the perverse patient as relying on omnipotent claims that there are no limits to what is possible sexually in an unconscious effort to shield himself from the frightening awareness of sexual and generational difference. Malcolm (1970) has clinically illustrated the idea that the analysis of perversion is not a matter of the dissection of the symbolism of deviant sexual acts, but the analysis of the experience of the perversion of the transference as it evolves in the analytic relationship (see also Meltzer 1973). More recently, Joseph (1994) has understood perverse sexual excitement in the analytic setting as a form of attack on the capacity of the analyst and analysand to think by means of a persistent sexualization of the transference and the act of thinking.

My focus in the clinical discussion that will follow will be on technical problems presented by the perversion of analytic intersubjectivity itself. I shall discuss the challenge to the analyst posed by his attempt to derive understanding of the perverse analytic process from his experience within it while still maintaining his capacity to think and speak to himself about it and eventually to discuss his understandings with the patient in the form of verbal interpretation. The clinical discussion will be followed by an effort to make a set of theoretical statements about aspects of the structure of perversion.

Clinical Illustration: Through the Looking Glass

Ms. A. began our first session by telling me that she had
decided to consult with me because her marriage was a
"sham." She and her husband had not had sex for
more than five years. The patient told me that what disturbed her most was that she recently realized that the
situation did not bother her. In the past, everything
mattered terribly, but now that she was middle-aged
(she was 43 years old), nothing seemed to matter. Her
two children were in their late teens and had recently
left home for college. It seemed to me that although
Ms. A. was not lying to me during our initial several
meetings, there was much more to the story of why she
was seeking analysis than she was revealing. This, of
course, is always the case, but I had the distinct impression that I was being kept in the dark about rather specific important matters about which Ms. A. was
consciously aware. There was something about being
with her that reminded me of watching (or in fantasy,
being in) a detective movie. In particular, I thought of
Jack Nicholson and Faye Dunaway in *Chinatown* and
several movies with Humphrey Bogart and Lauren
Bacall, the names of which I could not remember. I was
intrigued by Ms. A. Her choice of words was imaginative and her way of speaking had a vitality that were at
odds with her description of herself as a lifeless, middle-aged woman.

   In the course of the first year of analysis, Ms. A. told
me about her childhood in Southern California. Her

father was a real estate developer who quickly became very wealthy, and then was forced into bankruptcy as a result of a series of events that were not clear to Ms. A. The patient's father never let the fact of his past bankruptcy be known to friends and colleagues and kept up appearances for a period of more than a decade while he accumulated an even larger real estate "empire" than the one he had previously held. Following the rebuilding of his empire, most of Ms. A.'s father's friends, clients, and business partners were people associated with the film industry. Once or twice a month, the patient's parents would hold large parties at their home, events that constituted the center of the life of the family. Both parents seemed continually to be "consumed": Ms. A.'s mother devoted herself to the preparations for the next party while the patient's father worked with "feverish intensity" on his next real estate deal.

At these social events at the patient's family's home, there was a great deal of heavy drinking and drug taking. Cross dressing and flaunting of "outrageous homosexuality" by some of the guests stood out vividly in the patient's memory. Ms. A. attended most of these parties and said that when she was not pretending to be an adult, she felt invisible ("as if there weren't a child present"). At times, she felt like a prop in one or another of the guests' displays of his or her "sensitivity to children." At other times, she was treated as a "mock adult" in such a way that she felt that she was the brunt of a joke, the point of which she did not understand. Very often she felt terribly bored by the "sheer predict-

ability of it all: everyone could be counted on to be per-
fectly in role."

Although the patient did not remember observing
or being the object of overt sexual behavior, she said
that she felt that there was "far too much kissing going
on." Ms. A. said that she learned over time that this type
of kissing was a "social affectation." Nonetheless, it felt
"yucky" to her. The patient described these parties with
a thinly disguised sense of pride. She would mention,
in passing, names of famous film celebrities who were
regular guests at the parties.

The image of the patient's parents that emerged
from Ms. A.'s description of her childhood was one in
which there seemed to be a couple single-mindedly
together in the partnership of creating an illusion of
being an integral part of an "in crowd" of wealthy,
glamorous people, while having almost nothing else to
do with one another or with their children. The
patient's mother suffered from chronic insomnia and
other "nervous conditions." In order not to disturb the
patient's father, she would read during the night in the
guest bedroom. It was not openly acknowledged that
the parents kept separate bedrooms for virtually the
entirety of their marriage. In fact, at the outset of analysis, Ms. A. herself was not fully conscious of her suspi-
cion that her mother's "insomnia" was very likely a ruse
for her parents' maintaining separate bedrooms.

A good deal of the manifest content of the first
year-and-a-half of analysis involved the elaboration of a
narrative of the patient's life, particularly her child-

hood. Ms. A. spoke entertainingly, but left me very little room to comment on what she was saying. There were practically no periods of silence lasting longer than a few seconds. The patient was apologetic about the fact that she was unable to remember her dreams.

Ms. A. was not a beautiful woman in a conventional sense, but there was a compelling, subtle sexuality in almost everything she said and did. I looked forward to seeing her each day and enjoyed hearing her stories. The patient met me in the waiting room with a warm smile that conveyed the feeling that she was glad to see me, but was by no means desperately dependent on me. Ms A. had a youthful independence about her that seemed to invite me to join her in her rebelliousness. She gave the impression that she just happened to be in the neighborhood and decided to drop by. At the same time, the patient adhered to the format of the analytic frame, rarely being late, paying punctually, and addressing me as "Dr. Ogden" when on the rare occasion she left a telephone message.

Persistent fantasies included the idea of my having a serious physical illness the nature of which she felt I was hiding from her. There were also fears of breaches of confidentiality, for instance, anxiety that I would talk with her husband if he were to angrily accuse me of engaging in an endless analysis for my own benefit or of encouraging the patient to leave him. These fantasies were discussed at length including the idea that I was not what I appeared to be and the idea that the patient might feel that she was deceiving me in some way. Moreover, the excitement of such a battle over the patient was discussed as well as the idea of my wishing to steal the patient away from her husband. However, these interpretations seemed mechanical to me. The flatness of these interpretations and the patient's response to them reflected a more general paucity of reflective thought in the analysis. The patient's cleverness and talent in telling an interesting story seemed to serve as a substitute for spontaneous, creative thinking. (I similarly felt the need to be clever and noticed that I would occasionally supply the name of a book or a poem that the patient had momentarily forgotten.)

I attempted to attend to my own "reveries" (Bion, 1962a) during the sessions since I consider this aspect of the analytic experience to be indispensable to the understanding of the transference-countertransference (Ogden 1989b, 1994a, b, c, d). During one of these meetings, the patient was talking about having watched a television program with her husband the previous night. She described how the two of them had sat next to one another on their living room couch in a way that had felt to her like two strangers on a subway train sitting next to one another without the slightest feeling of connection between them. As Ms. A. was talking I found myself thinking about the fact that the attendant in the parking lot immediately next to my office building had begun making preparations to open a car wash in the parking lot. He had recently purchased a commercial vacuum cleaner that made a deafening noise when it was being used. His girlfriend, whom I found to be brassy and abrasive, was helping with the project. I imagined calling City Hall to file a complaint about violations of zoning ordinances concerning noise. Were there such ordinances? How could there not be? Is there nobody at City Hall with whom I could discuss this? There must be some kind of appeals process. I became increasingly anxious as I imagined this unreasonable, unapproachable couple and the bureaucratic maze at City Hall with nobody at the center of it.

As I emerged from this increasingly ruminative set of thoughts, feelings, and sensations, I was struck by the intensity of the anxiety that I was feeling.[2] I wondered about the parallels between the couple in the parking lot and the patient's parents, each pair with their plans that neither the patient nor I had the power to influence. I hypothesized that the idea of the frightening, disturbing noise of the vacuum cleaner might be related to a fantasy of noise coming from the parents' bedroom, the disturbing noise of an intercourse that was both empty (a vacuum) and consuming (sucking into it

---

2. Since it requires a considerable span of time to describe the experience of a reverie, the rhythm of the analysis is not well represented in my efforts at describing it in a linear fashion. The thoughts, feelings, and sensations involved in a reverie may occupy only a few moments. Consequently, it is inaccurate to think of the analyst's use of his reveries as reflecting a detached, self-absorbed, inattentive psychological state. On the contrary, the analyst's attentiveness to his own affective state as generated in the context of the analytic intersubjectivity contributes to a feeling of intense emotional immediacy and a sense of the analyst's resonance with the patient's unconscious experience in the present moment.

the patient's internal object world). My hypotheses concerning the connection between the elements of the
reverie and my experience in being with the patient
seemed strained and intellectualized. Nevertheless, the
reverie left me feeling extremely uneasy and alerted me
to the fact that I was feeling disturbed by something that
was occurring between the patient and me.

In the period of months following the session just
described, I very gradually began to recognize a sense
of pride that I had begun to take in the idea that other
people might know that I was Ms. A.'s analyst. I both
took pleasure in this fantasy and felt deeply ashamed of
it (and managed to keep it out of conscious awareness
almost completely). Ms. A. wore a great many different
hats, coats, and scarves and I found myself feeling
interested in what she would be wearing to each day's
session. As she entered the office, she would lay her
coat on the floor next to the couch (almost at my feet).
The designer label would often be in view and I would
have to strain to attempt to read it (upside down). (I
should emphasize that the countertransference[3] feel-

---

3. I use the term *countertransference* to refer to the analyst's
experience of and contribution to the transference-countertransference. As discussed above, the transference-countertransference
is understood as an unconscious intersubjective construction
experienced separately and individually by analyst and analysand. I
do not conceive of transference and countertransference as separable psychological entities that arise independently of, or in
response to one another, but as aspects of a single intersubjective
totality (Loewald 1986, Ogden 1994a, d).

ings that I am describing comprised a silent background that had not yet become a focus of conscious analysis. In other words, these aspects of the analysis had not yet become "analytic objects" [Bion 1962a, Green 1975, Ogden 1994a, b, c], i.e., elements of inter-subjective experience that were utilizable in the process of generating analytic meaning. Instead, this set of thoughts, feelings, and sensations remained a part of a largely unconscious intersubjective field in which I was, at that juncture, more participant than observer.)

It is often difficult to say what contributes to a shift in the balance of psychological-interpersonal forces that makes such background experience available for conscious use as analytic data. In the phase of work under discussion, it was in part a further set of anxiety-laden reveries (in association with the reveries previously described) that allowed aspects of heretofore largely unconscious background experience to begin to be transformed into "analytic objects." Initially, my anxiety was diffuse and centered on the feeling that I would be forgetful. I experienced a sense of pressure to remember to send a card to a relative whose birthday was approaching. I had changed a patient's appointment time and felt anxious that I would not be there at the correct time. I noticed that these passing thoughts during the session with Ms. A. were related to the feeling that there were "holes" in my consciousness. I wondered what it was that I was blinding myself to in the work with Ms. A. The anxiety was now real and immediate, although non-specific: its

meaning in relation to the leading unconscious transference anxieties was still unclear to me. However, a
shift in the quality of my self-awareness in the transference-countertransference was taking place.

Over the succeeding weeks of analysis, my anxiety
took on increasing specificity. I began to experience
anxiety just before the meetings with Ms. A., feeling
extremely awkward and self-conscious. Meeting her in
the waiting room felt like the beginning of a date. Ms.
A. seemed not to be experiencing anxiety of this sort
and, if anything, appeared to be all the more graceful
and fluid in her way of carrying herself, speaking, dressing, and so on.

It was during this period of analysis that the
patient presented the following dream:

> An old man was sitting in his study reading. It was
> like your office, but it wasn't actually your office. It
> was dark and had a dank, seedy feeling to it. Peo-
> ple were peering through the window at him. I was
> one of them. It was terribly important to be per-
> fectly still so as not to be caught. I was afraid I
> would pee. He seemed like a depressed, dirty old
> man. I thought he was only pretending to read or
> forcing himself to read. I also had the feeling that
> he was trying to turn himself on sexually by read-
> ing, but it wasn't working. I'm not sure if I thought
> this in the dream or as I was waking up, but it felt
> as if he knew how badly I needed to pee.

It was at this point that the very disturbing thought occurred to me that Ms. A. must have been watching me watch her. (The dream was about the excitement of secretly observing and about being observed in the act of secretly and excitedly watching and about the uncertainty of who was observing whom.) She must have known that I had tried to read the labels on her coats that she had draped at my feet. How long had she known? I felt intense embarrassment at the idea of having been observed looking. Everything seemed to have suddenly and unexpectedly been reversed: what had been private had become public; what had felt like simple curiosity had become prurient interest; the patient's nonchalance had taken on a feeling of manipulative control; what had felt like intimacy now felt like an experience of having been played for a fool.

For a moment, it seemed to me as if a trap had been carefully set and I had sprung it, but I also understood that I had been part of setting it. My having sprung the trap was not the thing that was the most humiliating part of all this to me. My feelings of embarrassment centered on the idea that I had sprung the trap long ago and had been unaware of it. I felt as if my own looking (which now felt like voyeurism) had been observed at every step. My secret had never been a secret. In addition, there was an intense feeling of betrayal.

I could now fully acknowledge to myself for the first time that I had unconsciously felt pride, pleasure, and guilt at having been included in an erotized duet with Ms. A. In the instant of recognition that I am describing, the experience of playing a role in this scene became transformed from an experience in which I had felt like an adult into an experience of myself as caught in the act of being a self-deceiving infant or child. My immaturity had been unmasked. I felt outside of adult sexuality with my nose pressed against the glass as represented in the dream by the patient's peering through the window in the dream while experiencing an infantile (urinary) form of sexual excitement.

At this juncture, I began to be able to talk to myself in a fuller way about my experience in the transference-countertransference. It seemed that a shared unconscious construction had been created in the analysis through which the patient had been giving shape to important aspects of her internal object world. It appeared that the intense embarrassment that I was feeling represented a disavowed and projected version of the patient's humiliation at finding herself to be an infantile onlooker in relation to her parents' (degraded) intercourse (which was in part equated with "the parties"). (Less consciously, the parents were felt to be excitedly observing her excitement.) I had experienced both the illusion/delusion of being a participant in the parental intercourse and the humiliation of being revealed to be *only an infant* who was excitedly pretending to be part of the primal scene.

Ms. A. and I in the (asymmetrically) shared experience of this transference-countertransference drama,
had each in our own way insisted that we were not the
outsider to the parental intercourse, but were "really"
adults participating in it. At this point, I began to
understand the patient's dream as reflecting an aspect
of Ms. A.'s internal object world about which I had
been only subliminally aware: the image of the intercourse in the dream was of a dead intercourse. The old
man (simultaneously representing me, the patient's
internal world, and the analytic relationship) was
depressed and lonely, going through the motions of
reading or perhaps attempting to escape his depression
by means of solitary, empty sexual excitement.

As I "emerged" from my reverie and subsequent
thoughts, I attempted to re-focus on what the patient
was saying. Of course, I was not returning to "a place
where we had left off," but to a "place" that had not
previously existed. Ms. A. at first spoke about her
dream by connecting her perennial fears of my being
ill with the fact that in the dream, the illness was a
depression. She then said that the dream reminded her
of something that had happened in the waiting room at
the beginning of the session. She told me that she
looked at me to see if I was tired or sick by checking to
see if I had dark circles under my eyes. She had hoped
that I had not seen her looking at me "in that way."

The patient then abruptly changed the topic. I
asked her if she had felt anxious when she cut herself
off in the middle of her observations and feelings about

what she had observed in the waiting room. She said, "I feel all over the place. It felt dangerous to be so specific about looking at you." (It seemed to me that the patient was unconsciously attempting [in an anxious and ambivalent way] to talk to me about the dangers of the exciting drama of looking and being looked at that had been enacted in the analysis and which were being depicted in the dream.)

I said that I thought that Ms. A. had experienced herself as being in more than one place at the same time in the dream and perhaps also in the relationship with me. Although she had in part experienced herself as one of the people looking through the window, it seemed to me that she was also identified with the dirty old man in my office and was observing him in the act of excitedly watching her. (The connection between the old man and me in the dream was so apparent that I did not feel it necessary to spell it out.)

I said to Ms. A. that she had linked the dream to her having stolen a look at me in the waiting room. I told her that I thought that for some time, she had both wanted me to understand and was afraid that I would understand the importance of a particular type of secretive looking that felt shameful to her. I said that I thought that she was trying to show me in the dream that she felt that an aspect of our relationship involved a kind of excitement that was connected with the experience of secretly looking and being caught in the act of excitedly watching. (I chose not to be more specific at this moment about the enactments in the analytic setting in order not to enter into another form of sado-masochistic activity.) The interpretation led to a palpable sense of relief on the part of both the patient and myself. Ms. A. was silent for several minutes after I made my comments (the first period of extended silence that had occurred in the analysis). During the silence, I felt relaxed in a way that I had not previously felt with Ms. A.

The patient then told me that what I had said had made her feel "understood, but not exposed, if that distinction makes sense." She said she would have expected to have felt painfully embarrassed by having this aspect of her spoken about by me. She was silent for the remaining few minutes of the session.

Ms. A. began the following meeting by saying that she had had a dream the previous night. In it she was herself as a child. She woke up in the dream to find that she had polio (a disease about which she had been quite phobic from the time she was a small child). On waking (in the dream) she could not move her legs, nor did she have any feeling in them. She was both extremely frightened and surprisingly calm. She imagined that she would never again be able to move her legs or have sensation in them.

The patient said that she felt the dream was a response to what had happened in our session the previous day. She said that the dream had been quiet in a way that reminded her of the silences in our meeting. The feeling in the dream was also a very odd combination of terror and relief connected with the fact that

the thing that she had most feared had finally happened. I thought of Winnicott's (1974) notion that the
dreaded event (the fear of breakdown) is an event that
has already occurred, but has not yet been experienced. I also thought, but did not say, that the patient's
emotional/sensory deadness (paralysis and loss of sensation) was beginning to be acknowledged without
immediately being buried in entertaining stories: the
silence for the moment, was not being filled with noise.
It seemed that the patient was evidencing the rudiments of the capacity to observe and to be able to think
about what she was experiencing, i.e., her sense of
deadness. There was for now an aspect of her (represented by the sensing/non-paralyzed part of her in the
dream) that paradoxically could feel the deadness of
another aspect of her and experience the lie (the
noise) as a lie.

It is not possible in the space of this chapter to
describe in detail the events of the analysis over the succeeding months and years. The transference-countertransference shift just described was followed by a
discussion of the central role in the analysis of the
patient's experience of secretly looking at me in a sexually exciting way and her fantasy of secretly, excitedly,
dangerously observing me in the act of excitedly
observing her. Gradually, in the course of this period of
work, details of the acting-in (for example, the patient's
observing me observe her laying her clothes at my feet)
were discussed. Again, these discussions were not conducted in a way that served to create the effect of an

embarrassing/exciting undressing of the patient, the analyst, or the analysis. Instead, the predominant feeling was that of the patient's loneliness and hopelessness about ever being able to experience herself as other than a "made up person."

Ms. A. began to understand the ways in which the elements of the perverse defense had been invaluable in protecting her from an experience of deadness that she had feared would be unbearable. In the course of the analysis, the patient described aspects of her life to which she had previously alluded, but had hardly existed in the analysis as "analytic objects," i.e., as events that carried meaning that could be experienced, noticed, considered, and thought about in the context of the network of meanings that were being elaborated. It would be inaccurate to say that these perceptions of past events had been unconscious or had been consciously withheld; rather, these largely unspoken aspects of her life (that will be discussed) had felt so disconnected from the entertaining storytelling that "it just never occurred to me to talk about these things." (See Freud [1927] for a discussion of the process of radical psychic disconnection involved in perversion. An analogous form of splitting was reflected in the countertransference experience of being "in the dark," "flying blind," and having "holes" in my consciousness.)

Over time, Ms. A. told me that from the time she was a child, she felt "consumed" by the need to get people, both boys and girls, men and women, to find her mysterious and sexy. It became a "full blown obsession" in high school to get boys to "chase her." "Everywhere I was and in everything I did, I was looking out of the corner of my eye to see who was looking at me."

Ms. A. had been extremely promiscuous in adolescence. In high school, she thought of herself as a "liberated rebel," but it became distressing over time to feel that she was driven by something that she could not control. Moreover, she was unable to speak to anyone about feeling out of control, which led her to feel intensely lonely. Ms. A. attempted to compensate for her sense of isolation by never being alone. She recalled talking with friends in college well into the night until they finally fell asleep, at which point the patient would sleep on their floor.

During this period of promiscuity and isolation, the patient was almost completely unable to think or talk with herself or with anyone else about what was happening to her. Instead, what might have become a thought or a feeling was experienced as extreme muscular tension in combination with a variety of psychosomatic illnesses including chronic amenorrhea, dermatitis, and severe headaches. Ms. A. said that she was unable to read or concentrate and managed her schoolwork by frequently cheating on exams and plagiarizing the work of other students. The cheating itself became exciting. Ms. A. took pleasure in "showing off" to her friends the risks that she was taking.

The patient said that she felt a mixture of shame and pride as she told me about her exploits. She told me that what made it easy to be so daring was that, "I genuinely did not give a shit if I were caught. What could they do to me?" Ms. A.'s choice of words surprised me in that she had not previously used scatological language. I wondered (silently) if she imagined that not having a body that needed to engage in ordinary human functions such as defecation ("not giving a shit") would provide her with a way of escaping from the emotional and bodily trap in which she felt caught and in danger of being psychically killed. I later suggested (in small bits over several weeks) that Ms. A. was indirectly telling me that her defiant claim to be alive "outside the system" (beyond the law and outside of her body), had been for a long time an important way of attempting to protect herself from being taken over by the internal lives of other people. I said that it seemed that she had felt terribly privileged and special while at the same time feeling as if she were ceasing "to be anybody." The patient began to recognize the profound confusion that she had felt about whose desire it was that was fueling her wish/need to be at parties. It no longer seemed possible to separate out in any meaningful way her own desires from those of others. The transference implications of these recognitions were explored including the confusion about whose sexual excitement was whose in the dream as well as in the transference-countertransference events that had occurred in the analysis.

In discussing this set of feelings, the patient became aware of the way in which it had served her defensively to create the illusion that the power to "do anything" she wished set her apart from everyone else. The anxiety associated with the confusion of not knowing whose desire it was that she was experiencing was somewhat allayed by the illusion that she "occupied a different universe from everyone else." Ms. A. came to understand that hidden by her sense of power was an unconscious feeling of impotence (paralysis) to think, feel, and behave outside of the terms of her exploits, machinations, and manipulations. Hers was a world of unreflective action and reaction. Ms. A. said that there had been periods of her life, especially during the latter years of college, during which she had for brief periods recognized the bizarre nature of the way she was living and felt horrified by it and deeply ashamed of it. Although she had a great many sexual experiences, she felt bored by the sex. During intercourse she felt as if she were watching what was happening in a way that felt like "watching a television program that wasn't very interesting." Ms. A. at times became disturbingly aware of the inhuman quality of this and other aspects of her life. However, the feeling of despair associated with these moments of self-awareness was short-lived.

During the phase of work in which this narrative and set of understandings unfolded, I felt an increasing sense of continuity between the content of Ms. A.'s verbal symbolization and the matrix of the transference-countertransference (Ogden, 1991a). The initial years of the analysis had, in retrospect, been marked by a discontinuity of manifest and latent, of verbal content and experiential context. The manifest and acknowledged aspect of the analytic relationship had been quite disconnected from a troubling, exciting "second narrative" that resisted symbolization, and instead remained a powerful, erotized (predominantly unconscious) intersubjective construction.

Discussion

Ms. A.'s very first statement to me was about her marriage (unconsciously, her life) being a "sham." It took a long time for me to understand in any depth what it was that she was unconsciously attempting to tell me. From the outset, there was a subliminal seductive coyness to Ms. A.'s presentation of herself. There was also a quality of mystery conveyed by all that was not being said, which contributed to my feeling of being "in the dark," perhaps unconsciously in a darkened bedroom. In retrospect, my initial thoughts about the patient and me as characters in a detective film can be understood as a reflection of my then unconscious sense that the analytic relationship was being constructed on a foundation involving a confusing mixture of grandiose erotized fantasy, prevarication, self-deception, and the background theme of a perverse primal scene (the sadomasochistic incestuous relationship depicted in *Chinatown*).

I had found the patient's accounts of her childhood (her stories) to be not only interesting, but often fascinating. There was a way in which the patient continued to be captivated (and captivating) by her experience of having occupied a privileged position in which she could pose as a child while not feeling like a child in a secret world of adult sexual excitement and exhibitionism. She observed and participated in (from a distance) the "parties" (that were unconsciously equated with the primal scene). The patient felt that no ordinary child would be allowed to have knowledge of, much less see, hear, smell, or touch these extraordinary events. Ms. A. imagined that she knew important and frightening secrets, for example, the secret of her father's financial, sexual, emotional bankruptcy and the secret that some people had succeeded in remaining both male and female (as represented by the homosexuality and cross-dressing that she observed and vividly remembered).

Less conscious to the patient in her initial accounts of her childhood was the central role of the illusion of her not being "only a child," and instead being a part of an adult intercourse in which she (in identification with the homosexual and transvestite figures), was not limited to being a member of a single sex nor fixed in a single generation (see Chasseguet-Smirgel 1984).

As exciting as Ms. A. found the adult discourse/intercourse which she observed and which she (in fantasy) participated, the intercourse was at the same time experienced as dead. The patient unconsciously knew of her parents' separate sleeping arrangements and sensed the emptiness of the partially drug-induced, hypomanic, exhibitionistic sexual scene which she found to be frightening, repulsive, other worldly, and yet repetitive and tedious. This paradoxical flatness of the "exciting" experience represented a powerful element of the transference-countertransference. Both the patient and I attempted to disguise and enliven the persistent absence of spontaneous thought in the analysis with unconsciously erotized cleverness, for example, the pressure to which both the patient and I were responding in our name dropping and in the effort to use "just the right, knowing phrase."

My reverie about the opening of the car wash in the parking lot provided an important medium through which to experience elements of the transference-countertransference that had been present from early on, but had been very little available to either Ms. A. or to me for generating verbally symbolized analytic meaning. My reverie involved the fantasy of a loud vacuum cleaner being operated by a diabolical couple from whom I was helplessly cut off. The couple seemed to operate in a realm that was above the law and beyond the reach of words and human emotion. In the reverie, not only was there no law at City Hall, there was no human presence at its core.

This reverie represented an important development in the evolution of the analytic process in that it allowed me something of a foothold in a perspective that was both outside of, and yet informed by, the inter-subjective construction in which I was participating (the perverse subject of analysis).

The meaning of the "car wash reverie" felt quite disconnected from my experience in the transference-countertransference and yet the reverie had a profoundly disturbing effect on me and led me to be alert in a qualitatively different way to what I was experiencing with this patient. I began to notice (with a considerable degree of shame) both the pride that I was feeling in being Ms. A.'s analyst (the pleasure in "being seen with her") and the pleasure I was taking in observing her clothes that were being laid at my feet. At the same time, I became aware of the feeling of a "hole" or blind spot in my awareness that made me feel all the more that I was blinding himself to something important in my role as analyst for Ms. A. (See Steiner [1985] for a discussion of the meanings of "turning a blind eye" in the Oedipus myth.)

The accretion of experiences that I have described led the rather diffuse anxiety that I had been experiencing to be transformed into a much more clearly defined and consciously articulated sexual anxiety (associated with seeing and being seen). I experienced this anxiety in the form of the unsettling (conscious) fantasy that each time I encountered Ms. A. in the waiting room I was meeting her for a date.

The patient's telling me her dream of the observed man served to crystallize several powerful unconscious constellations of meaning that had structured the experience of the transference-countertransference to that point. Despite my feeling of sudden recognition, my awareness of the pivotal importance of the experience of secretly observing and being observed had been developing over a rather long period of time (as reflected in my reveries). When the patient told me her dream, a marked affective shift occurred. What I had previously experienced as ideas about erotized observing and being observed now became a detailed, visceral knowledge of the experience of being caught in the act of a particular form of curious, sexualized looking. The nature of the exposure involved in the transference-countertransference event was the exposure of the infant/child excitedly observing (and in fantasy participating in) the primal scene. My feelings of shame associated with this act derived in large part from the feeling of being revealed to be a presumptuous and self-deceptive infant/child pretending to be an adult participant in the primal scene.

The transference-countertransference experience being discussed was not simply an experience of being painfully exposed; it was equally an (unconscious) experience of excitedly tempting the observer and then exposing the observer to be the excluded infant/child that he or she is. Fundamental to the patient's experience of "catching the observer in the act" was her defensive disavowal, splitting off and projection of her feelings of being the envious, excluded, curious, sexually aroused, self-deceptive infant. Moreover, Ms. A.'s act of tempting me in the way described was a source of excitement in itself in that there was the ever-present danger of her being "caught in the act" of secretly observing me observing her. It must be remembered that all of this was occurring in the context of what was otherwise a dead discourse/intercourse (non-self-reflective "reporting" and "storytelling" that was almost entirely devoid of spontaneous, creative thought). In this light, the "excitement" of the exciting/dangerous game being described represented an unconscious effort to create a substitute for a genuinely creative discourse/intercourse. The patient's dream imagery underscored the deadness of the intercourse: the depressed old man in a dark room was only going through the motions of reading and was (unsuccessfully) attempting to use sexual excitement to distract himself from his emptiness and depression. The excitement/danger in the dream (partially experienced as the sensation of being on the verge of involuntary urination) lay in the act of secretly observing the man (his symbolic intercourse) and in secretly being observed in the act of observing. The interpretations that I offered at this point were informed by my experiences in and of the perverse transference-countertransference, which experiences allowed me to understand and feel compassion for both the exposed and the exposing aspects of the internal object relationship that so dominated the patient's life and the life of the analysis.

The patient then became engaged in the process of "retelling a life" (Schafer 1994), not in the sense of telling it again, but in the sense of recasting the past in the context of a new set of intersubjective experiences that had occurred in the transference-countertransference and were in the process of occurring in the analysis. A new narrative was generated by the patient that held a form of coherence of past and present that was rooted in a less fearful, less anxiously self-deceptive experience of herself and her relations with others. In this period of work, Ms. A. evidenced a capacity for reflective thought. Words were no longer primarily a medium for creating a Siren song and instead were used as a vehicle for participating in an analytic discourse shaped by the recognition of roles of analyst and analysand. In addition, the patient evidenced for the first time, the beginnings of a capacity to contain (live with) her fear of deadness (as represented in her dream of being paralyzed and without sensation in her legs) that she had so strenuously attempted to mask through the use of defensive sexualization. Silence could now be tolerated rather than being immediately transformed into the "noise" of the erotized, magnetic storytelling.

At the same time, it must be emphasized that the analytic movement being described reflects only the beginnings of what would eventually become a more stable set of psychological changes. The defensive pseudo-maturity involved in the perverse excitement of the initial stages of analysis were followed by other forms of defense against the feeling of humiliation of being "only an infant" in a confusing/frightening/exciting/dead adult world. For example, in the course of Ms. A.'s telling me about the ways in which she felt "possessed" in adolescence and as a young adult, the transference (as "total situation" [Klein 1952, Joseph 1985, Ogden 1991a]) involved a sense of anxiously pressured collegiality in which there was an effort to deny generational and role differences in the analytic relationship. Moreover, intellectualization was used to protect the patient from feelings of not knowing, of "being in the dark." Although the transference anxieties being warded off were similar in nature to those experienced in the earlier stages of work, the perversion of the transference-countertransference no longer constituted the principal medium of communication, defense, and object relatedness.

Before leaving the clinical portion of the chapter, I would like to briefly elaborate an idea that has been implicit in the foregoing discussion. An element of technique that is reflected in the analysis that has been described is the analyst's use of his mundane, unobtrusive, quotidian thoughts, feelings, sensations, fantasies, daydreams, ruminations, and so on in the process of attempting to understand the network of intersubjectively generated meanings constituting the transference-countertransference. The experience of understanding that evolved in the portion of the analysis just described had the quality of a disturbing recognition, a sense of sudden reversal. This quality of psychological movement (i.e., an unsettling recognition of a formerly split off unconscious discourse) reflected the nature of the perverse process and its precarious, potentially explosive tension between honesty and deception, intimacy and manipulation, the authentic and the counterfeit. It is important to bear in mind that the use of reverie in the understanding of the transference-countertransference is usually a much "quieter" process and does not often lead to such dramatic shifts in perspective or feelings of shameful self-deception.

Some Theoretical Comments

Building upon the understanding of aspects of the perverse transference-countertransference discussed above, as well as my experience in analyzing similar transference-countertransference enactments in work with other patients (Ogden 1994b), I shall offer some tentative thoughts about what I believe to be important elements of the structure of this form of perversion. The perverse individual of the type being discussed experiences a sense of inner deadness, a lack of a sense of being alive as a human being (Khan 1979, McDougall 1978, 1986); at the same time, there develops a set of concretely symbolized defensive fantasies that life exists in the intercourse (both sexual and non-sexual) between the parents and that the only way to "acquire" life is to enter into that intercourse (the source of life) from which the individual is excluded and left lifeless (Britton 1989, Klein 1926, 1928, Meltzer 1973, O'Shaughnessy 1989). Of course, in a literal way, it is the parental intercourse that is the source of the patient's life, but this biological fact has for the perverse patient failed to become a psychological fact.

At the same time, these perverse patients fantasize/experience the parental intercourse (in the broadest sense of the word) to be an empty event, and imagine that the lifelessness of the primal scene is the source of his or her own sense of inner deadness. In part, this fantasy is based on the patient's own envious attack on the parental intercourse. It also reflects the patient's experience (a combination of perception and fantasy) of the emptiness of the bond between the parents. This perception/fantasy of an absence at the core of human discourse/intercourse leaves these perverse individuals feeling that there is no hope of attaining a sense of vitality of their own internal world and in their relations with external objects. What is particular to perversion of the sort being discussed is the compulsive erotization of the void that is felt at the center of what might have been, and pretends to be, a generative union between the parents. The excitement generated by this erotization is used as a substitute for a sense of one's own human aliveness as well as the recognition of the humanness of other people. This erotic substitution is unconsciously experienced as a lie, and other people are compulsively enlisted in the enactment of this sexualized lie.

The unconsciously fantasied empty parental intercourse is defensively rendered exciting in part by attributing to it the feeling of danger. These perverse patients repeatedly and compulsively enlist others in the process of enacting the fantasy of entering into the parental intercourse which enactments are felt to involve a threat to the patient's life (McDougall 1986). There is at the same time a critical act of self-deception that allows the patient to isolate himself from awareness of the reality of the danger to which he is subjecting himself. The individual deludes himself and prides himself in his belief that he is able to "fly closer to the flame" than anybody else without being damaged. He or she believes him or herself to be immune to all danger while at the same time being intensely excited by it. The desperate need to extract life from (and infuse life into) the empty parental intercourse leads the patient to flaunt external reality and (unconsciously) claim to exist outside of the law (including both the laws of society and the laws of nature) (Chasseguet-Smirgel 1984). Since the individual's psychological life has in a sense already been lost (or more accurately, has never come into being), there is a certain reality to the idea that he has nothing to lose.

The foregoing comments might be briefly stated in the form of the following set of schematic propositions:

1. In healthy development a sense of oneself as alive is equated with a generative loving parental intercourse. Out of this intercourse comes a feeling of aliveness from which the patient derives a sense of the vitality and realness of his or her own thoughts, feelings, sensations, subjectivity, object relations, and so on.

2. Perversion of the type being discussed represents an endless, futile effort to extract life from a primal scene that is experienced as dead.

3. Perversion of this sort involves a form of excitement derived from the cynical subversion of the (purported) truth of the aliveness of the parental intercourse which source of vitality is felt to be inaccessible and probably nonexistent. In other words, the seemingly generative, loving

parental intercourse is felt to be a lie, a hoax.
These perverse individuals introject a fantasied
degraded intercourse and subsequently engage
others in a compulsively repeated acting out of
this set of internal object relationships.

4. In this form of perversion, a vicious cycle is gen-
    erated in which the fantasied intercourse of the
    parents is depicted as loveless, lifeless and non-
    procreative; the patient attempts (in vain) to
    infuse it with pseudo-excitement from which he
    attempts to extract life (or more accurately,
    attempts to create a substitute for life). Since the
    fantasied parental intercourse from which the
    perverse patient is attempting to extract life is
    experienced as dead, he or she is attempting to
    extract life from death, truth from falsehood.
    Alternatively, the patient may attempt to use the
    lie as a substitute for truth/life (Chasseguet-
    Smirgel 1984).

5. An important method of attempting to infuse
    the empty primal scene with life (excitement
    and other substitutes for feelings of aliveness) is
    the experience of "flirting with danger," tempt-
    ing fate by "flying too close to the flame."

6. The desire of these perverse individuals is co-
    opted by and confused with the desire of others
    leading them more deeply into defensive mis-
    recognitions and misnamings of their experi-
    ence in order to create the illusion of self-
    generated desire (Ogden 1988a).

7. Analysis of perversion, as clinically illustrated in this chapter, fundamentally involves recognizing (naming accurately) the lie/lifelessness that constitutes the core of the transference-counter-transference enactment of the perversion. In this way, the patient, perhaps for the first time in his or her life, feels engaged in a discourse that is experienced as alive and real.

8. The initial feelings of aliveness and realness in the analysis arise from the recognition of the lifelessness/lie of the transference-countertrans-ference and consequently are most often fright-ening feelings of deadness. This experience is different from the deadness of the lie/lifeless-ness that had not been recognized as a lie and which had been masquerading as truth. For-merly, the lie (the empty intercourse) had to be infused with false/perverse excitement in an effort to bring life to it and acquire life from it. The recognition of the lie is not an experience of sexual excitement but makes possible a state of mind in which sexual aliveness (in the con-text of whole object relations) and generative thinking and discourse might be experienced.

Concluding Comments

In this chapter, I have clinically illustrated the way in which the analysis of perversion necessarily involves the elaboration of an unconscious perverse transference-countertransference which is contributed to and participated in by both analyst and analysand. This intersubjective construction is powerfully shaped by the perverse structure of the patient's unconscious internal object world. The analyst's understanding of the perverse enactment in which he or she is an unwitting participant is developed in part through the elaboration and analysis of unobtrusive quotidian thoughts, feelings, fantasies, daydreams, ruminations, sensations, and so on, which are often seemingly unrelated to the patient. Understandings developed in this way are utilized in the process of the formulation of transference interpretations.

—— *4* ——

Privacy, Reverie, and Analytic Technique

*I hold this to be the highest task of two
people: that each should stand guard over
the solitude of the other.*

R. M. Rilke, 1904

Debussy felt that music is the space between the notes.
Something similar might be said of psychoanalysis.
Between the notes of the spoken words constituting the
analytic dialogue are the reveries of the analyst and the
analysand. It is in this space occupied by the interplay
of reveries that one finds the music of psychoanalysis.
The current chapter represents an effort to examine
some of the methods (techniques) that we as analysts
depend upon to help us listen to this music.

In this chapter and the next, I shall attempt to
describe three separate, but interrelated implications
for psychoanalytic technique that derive from the

understanding of the relationship among privacy, communication, and the experience of "the inter-subjective
analytic third" (Ogden 1992a, b, 1994a, b, c, d). As will
be discussed, I believe that the creation of an analytic
process depends upon the capacity of analyst and
analysand to engage in a dialectical interplay of states
of "reverie" (Bion, 1962a) that are at the same time private and unconsciously communicative.

After briefly discussing the concept of the analytic third, I shall address the role of the use of the
couch as a component of the analytic framework.
This will lead to a discussion of the question of the
relationship of the role of the couch to the frequency
of meetings.

I shall then propose that the "fundamental rule" of
psychoanalysis as introduced and described by Freud
(1900, 1912, 1913) fails to facilitate conditions in which
reveries might be generated by the analysand (and by
the analyst), and in fact often impedes the creation of
an analytic process. A reconceptualization of the fundamental rule will be suggested.

In the next chapter, I shall reconsider commonly
held beliefs about the handling of dreams in analysis
and shall suggest alternative approaches that are
founded upon a conception of the analytic process as a
dialectical interplay of subjectivities of analyst and
analysand resulting in the creation of an "intersubjective dream space." The dream dreamt in the course of
an analysis is in a sense the dream of the analytic third.
A fragment of analytic work will be presented in which

a dream is conceptualized and responded to as a product of the intersubjective analytic dream space.

The Analytic Third

Over the past several years, I have developed a conception of the analytic process that is based on the idea that in addition to the analyst and analysand, there is a third subject of analysis to which I have referred as "the intersubjective analytic third" or simply "the analytic third" (Ogden 1992a, b, 1994a, b, c, d). (See Baranger 1993, and Green 1975, for related conceptions of analytic intersubjectivity.) The (intersubjective) third subject of analysis stands in dialectical tension with the analyst and analysand as separate individuals with their own subjectivities. Analyst and analysand each participate in the unconscious intersubjective construction (the analytic third), but do so asymmetrically. Specifically, the relationship of the roles of analyst and analysand structures the analytic interaction in a way that strongly privileges the exploration of the unconscious internal object world of the analysand. This is so because most fundamentally the analytic relationship exists for the purpose of helping the analysand make psychological changes that will enable him to live his life in a more fully human way. The privileging of the exploration of the unconscious life of the analysand is effected through the analyst's use of his training and experience in the employment of his own unconscious in the service of being recep-

tive to the "drift" (Freud 1923a, p. 239) of the unconscious of the analysand.

The experience of patient and analyst in relation
to the intersubjective analytic third is asymmetrical not
only in terms of the way in which each contributes to its
construction and elaboration. It is also asymmetrical in
that analyst and analysand each experience the analytic
third in the context of his own separate, individual personality system which is shaped and structured by his
own form of psychological organization, his own layer-
ings and linkages of personal meanings derived from
the totality of his history and unique set of life experiences, his own modes of organizing and experiencing
bodily sensations, and so on. In sum, the analytic third
is not a single event experienced identically by two people; rather, it is a jointly, but asymmetrically constructed and experienced set of conscious and
unconscious intersubjective experiences in which analyst and analysand participate.

The Role of the Couch in the Analytic Process

In this portion of the discussion, I shall focus on some
implications for technique of the concept of the analytic third as it bears on a critical element of the analytic frame: the use of the couch.

In approaching the question of the role of the
couch as an aspect of the analytic framework, it is necessary to begin with the difficult question of what it is
that constitutes the essential elements of psychoanalysis

as a therapeutic process. The framework must serve the process and therefore, in order to determine whether an element of the framework does indeed facilitate a psychoanalytic process, one must attempt to broadly delineate for oneself the nature of the process.

It is clearly beyond the scope of the present chapter to offer a thorough discussion of the fundamental elements that constitute psychoanalysis as a therapeutic process. Instead, I shall simply offer some thoughts on the subject that might serve as a starting point for the exploration of this question. To do so I shall build upon Freud's conception of the essential elements that define psychoanalysis as a method of treatment. Freud (1914) held that "Any line of investigation which recognizes . . . these two facts [transference and resistance] and takes them as the starting-point of its work has a right to call itself psycho-analysis . . ." (p. 16). I would suggest the following elaboration of Freud's succinct statement. Perhaps psychoanalysis might be viewed as involving a recognition not only of transference and resistance, but also a recognition of the nature of the intersubjective field within which transference and resistance are generated. Specifically, as discussed above, I have in mind the creation of a third subject of analysis through which the phenomena of transference and resistance are given symbolic meaning on the analytic stage. That intersubjective construction (the analytic third) is generated through the dialectical interplay of the individual subjectivities of analyst and analysand in the context of their roles as analyst and analysand.

The problem of defining the nature of the role of
the couch as a component of the analytic framework
then becomes a problem of conceptualizing the role of
the use of the couch in the process of facilitating a state
of mind in which the intersubjective analytic third
might be generated, experienced, elaborated, and utilized by analyst and analysand. Utilizing experience in
and of the analytic third involves the creation of symbols in the analytic dialogue (predominantly, but not
exclusively verbal symbols) for heretofore unspeakable
and unthinkable aspects of the analysand's internal
object world.

Freud (1913) viewed "getting the patient to lie on
the sofa while I sit behind him out of sight" (p. 133) as
two essential, interrelated elements of the analytic set-
up which he said he "insists upon" (p. 134). Both the
patient's use of the couch and the analyst's being "out
of sight" allowed Freud to "give myself over to the current of my unconscious thoughts" (p. 134). Although
he originally introduced the use of the couch as a format designed to help the patient "to concentrate his
attention on his self-observation" (Freud 1900, p. 101),
Freud's (1911-1915) emphasis in his discussion of the
use of the couch in his *Papers on Technique* was not
on its role in facilitating the patient's capacity to free
associate. Rather, Freud's principal focus in these
papers was on the way in which the use of the couch
affords the analyst the privacy that he requires to do
his work: "I cannot put up with being stared at . . .
while I am listening to the patient . . ." (1913, p. 134).

This statement is often seen as a reflection of one of Freud's personal idiosyncracies or even as a manifestation of an aspect of his psychopathology. I believe that such readings fail to appreciate the great importance that Freud placed on the necessity of building into the structure of the analytic setting conditions in which the reveries of the analyst can be generated and utilized. Freud (1912) insisted that the task of the analyst is to "simply listen" (p. 112). I believe that the injunction to "simply listen" was Freud's highly condensed way of suggesting that the analyst attempt to render himself as unconsciously receptive as possible to the patient's unconscious and to attempt to avoid becoming mired in conscious (secondary process) efforts at organizing his experience.

In sum, Freud (1913) believed that the patient's use of the couch and the analyst's privacy in his position "out of sight" behind the couch are critical components of the supporting structure, "the framework" of psychoanalysis. Such an arrangement helps provide conditions of privacy in which the analyst might enter a state of reverie in which he gives himself "over to the current of [his] unconscious thoughts" (p. 134) and renders his own unconscious receptive to the unconscious of the analysand. Implicit in this discussion is the idea that the analysand in using the couch might also experience similar respite from being stared at and might more easily give himself over to the drift of his own unconscious thoughts (and perhaps also to those of the analyst).

Some Comments on Technique

When I introduce to the patient the idea of the use of
the couch in the beginning of an analysis, I explain to
the analysand that it is my practice to have the patient
lie on the couch while I sit in my chair behind the
couch. I go on to explain that I do so because I have
found that this arrangement affords me the privacy to
experience and think about what is occurring in a way
that is necessary for me to do the analytic work. I add
that the analysand may find that this way of working
also allows him to experience his own thoughts and
feelings in a way that feels to him different from his
ordinary ways of thinking, feeling, and experiencing
bodily sensations. Presenting the use of the couch in a
manner that emphasizes my own need as well as that of
the analysand for an area of privacy, a psychological
space (in both a literal and a metaphorical sense) in
which to think and generate experience, represents an
important statement to the patient of my conception of
the analytic method and of our overlapping roles in it.

It has been implicit in what has been said thus far
that I view the circumstances required for both analyst
and analysand to gain access to a state of reverie to be a
necessary condition for the conduct of analysis. One
might compare the necessary conditions for analysis to
the surgeon's requirement for a sterile field in which to
operate. In both the case of the analyst and of the surgeon, knowledge, training, and skillfulness of technique are liable to be rendered inconsequential if the

necessary context for the work does not exist. I have come to view the use of the couch as an important contributing element to the creation of the conditions in which reverie might be generated and utilized. At the same time, the patient's use of the couch (while the analyst sits behind it, out of sight) is but one set of factors contributing to the conditions that facilitate the creation of an analytic process. Moreover, the fact that the patient is using the couch is by no means a guarantee that an analytic process is being generated and utilized (See Goldberger [1995] for a discussion of the patient's use of the couch as a potential for transference enactment.)

The current discussion of the role of the couch in facilitating conditions for the elaboration of states of reverie is not meant to suggest that the analyst should insist (in a spoken or an unspoken manner) that every analytic patient use the couch at all times (Fenichel 1941, Frank 1995, Jacobson 1995, Lichtenberg 1995). There are periods of analysis when the use of the couch is too frightening for the patient to tolerate. Under these circumstances, it would be counter-therapeutic for the analyst to attempt to bypass the recognition and analysis of the patient's anxiety by pressuring him to use the couch. Such behavior on the part of the analyst would likely represent a form of countertransference acting-out.

The Couch in Analytic Practice

With the background of the preceding discussion of the use of the couch (including the analyst's position out of sight behind it) as a part of the analytic framework designed to make possible "overlapping state of reverie," I would like to turn to a brief consideration of a related question of analytic practice: Should analysts restrict the use of the couch to patients being seen four or more times a week? This question requires that we return to the matter of what we consider to be the elements that define an analytic process. Since analytic technique must facilitate the analytic process, the question becomes one of examining the role of the couch in facilitating the creation of an analytic process. In other words, does it seem that the nature of the analytic process as we understand it is tied to a specific frequency of meetings (for example, four or more meetings per week) or is the analytic process defined by a specific quality of psychological-interpersonal experience that may be independent of the frequency of meetings?

In an effort to begin to consider these interrelated questions, I shall schematically present a series of thoughts relating to my conception of the nature of the analytic process. The series of thoughts will ultimately address the relationship of the use of the couch to the frequency of meetings.

1. Psychoanalysis is a psychological-interpersonal process that requires conditions in which analyst

and analysand jointly (and asymmetrically) generate an unconscious third subject of analysis.

2. The analysis of unconscious (transference-countertransference) experience requires receptivity to states of reverie on the part of both analyst and analysand with which to recontextualize (more accurately, to newly contextualize) unconscious aspects of experience.

3. Associational linkages and new contextualizations among (largely) unconscious aspects of experience require that privacy conducive to a state of reverie be afforded to both analyst and analysand.

4. The patient's use of the couch (with the analyst seated out of sight behind the couch) fosters conditions in which analyst and analysand might each have sufficient privacy with which to enter into their own states of reverie, which states involve an area of "overlap." (*"Psychotherapy takes place in the overlap of two areas of playing, that of the patient and that of the therapist"* [Winnicott 1971a, p. 38].)

5. It then follows that the patient's use of the couch (and the analyst's privacy behind it) provide a means of facilitating access on the part of analyst and analysand to a "play space," an area of overlapping states of reverie, that is a necessary condition for the elaboration and analysis of the unconscious, intersubjective analytic third (cf. Grotstein 1995).

6. However else one defines analysis, it seems essential to include in one's definition the effort to
generate and experience the unconscious analytic third and to foster a state of reverie through
which the analyst and analysand might get a sense
of the "drift" (Freud 1923a) of that "shared" (and
yet individually experienced) unconscious construction. The analytic enterprise is best defined
not by its form (including the frequency of meetings), but by its substance, which involves the
analysis of the transference-countertransference
(including anxiety/defense) as these phenomena are given shape in the experiencing of and
interpretation of the analytic third.

It has been my experience that it is regularly the
case that increasing the frequency of sessions per week
enhances the capacity of analyst and analysand to generate overlapping states of reverie. To my mind, it
makes no sense to respond to a compromise of one set
of conditions under which an analysis is being conducted by compromising other conditions conducive
to the creation of an analytic process. Specifically, it
would be difficult for me to understand the logic
underlying a decision to work with a patient in a face-
to-face manner because conditions conducive to the
creation of an analytic process have been compromised
as a result of constraints leading to a frequency of meetings that seems to the analyst to be less than optimal. As
a result, unless there are compelling reasons not to use

the couch in a given instance, I conduct all of my analytic work with the patient using the couch, regardless of the number of times per week that the patient is being seen.[1]

Re-Casting the Fundamental Rule

Although the term "fundamental rule" was not introduced by Freud until 1912, the concept was always a central part of Freud's (1900) thinking about analytic technique in *The Interpretation of Dreams*. In 1913 Freud made his most fully elaborated statement regarding "the fundamental rule of psycho-analytic technique which the patient has to observe" (p. 134): "This must be imparted to him [the analysand] at the very beginning: 'One more thing before you start. What you tell me must differ in one respect from an ordinary conversation . . . You will be tempted to say to yourself that this or that is irrelevant here, or quite unimportant, or non-

---

1. My use of analytic technique in the service of generating an analytic process (for example, use of reverie in relation to my understanding of my experience of the transference-countertransference and my use of this understanding in the interpretation of the leading transference-countertransference anxiety) does not change in response to the number of times per week that I am seeing a patient. For example, I rely no more on suggestion, exhortation, reassurance, and the like in work with patients being seen once or twice per week than I do with patients being seen four, five, or six times per week.

sensical, so that there is no need to say it. You must never give in to these criticisms, but must say it spite of them—indeed, you must say it precisely *because* you feel an aversion to doing so . . . So say whatever goes through your mind . . . Finally, never forget that you have promised to be absolutely honest, and never leave anything out because, for some reason or other, it is unpleasant to tell it'" (pp.134–135).

A recent review of the literature (Lichtenberg and Galler 1987) revealed that "very few papers in the literature have as their main topic a modification in . . . the fundamental rule, and only slightly more suggest modifications in passing" (p.52). In a more fully elaborated commentary on the fundamental rule, Etchegoyen (1991) states: "Special circumstances can arise in which it is advisable to follow a path other than the usual one, without this meaning in any way that we can depart from the [fundamental] rule" (p. 65).

There are several aspects of the question of the fundamental rule that I shall address. It seems to me that any consideration of the role of the "fundamental rule" must begin by relating this aspect of technique to our conception of the analytic process as a whole since *technique must facilitate process*. Viewed very broadly, psychoanalysis might be described as a psychological-interpersonal process intended to enhance the analysand's capacity to be alive as a human being. Although a great many analysts have made pivotal contributions to this conception of analysis, Winnicott is perhaps the principal architect of a modern conception of psychoanalysis in which the central focus of the analytic process has been broadened from the task of making the unconscious conscious (in the language of the topographic model) or of transforming id into ego (in the language of the structural model). The analytic process for Winnicott (1971b) has as its central concern the expansion of the capacity of analyst and analysand to create "a place to live" in an area of experiencing that lies between reality and fantasy.

The psychoanalytic process, as conceived by Winnicott, demands of analytic technique a full appreciation of the importance of the generative tension between privacy and interpersonal relatedness: "Although healthy persons communicate and enjoy communicating, the other fact is equally true, that *each individual is an isolate, permanently non-communicating, permanently unknown, in fact, unfound.* . . . At the centre of each human being is an incommunicado element, and this is sacred and most worthy of preservation" (Winnicott 1963, p. 187).

On the basis of this conception of what it is to be human, Winnicott comments on psychoanalysis as a theory (although the implications of his comments for analytic technique are clear): "We can understand the hatred people have of psycho-analysis which has penetrated a long way into the human personality, and which provides a threat to the human individual in his need to be secretly isolated" (p. 187). A bit later, he adds, "We must ask ourselves, does our technique allow for the patient to communicate that he or she is not communicating?" (p. 188). It is this question that forms the backdrop for my own re-examination of the fundamental rule.

In previous contributions (Ogden 1989a, b, 1991b), I have discussed my own conception of the role of personal isolation in protecting the individual against the continuous strain that is an inescapable part of living in the unpredictable matrix of human object relations (1991b). I have emphasized the life-sustaining role of sensation-dominated ("autistic-contiguous" [1989a, b,])forms of experience in the creation of a temporary suspension of relatedness both to the mother/analyst as object and to the mother/analyst as environment. As a result of this view of the central role of privacy/personal isolation in healthy human experience, I do not in my own practice of analysis instruct the patient to attempt to say everything that comes to mind regardless of how "illogical or embarrassing or trivial or seemingly irrelevant" (Greenson 1971, p. 102) it may seem. Neither do I believe that it is sufficient to "soften" the fundamental rule with comments such as, "I understand that the task of saying everything that comes to mind is a difficult (or impossible) one."

Instead, it is my practice to simply invite the patient, in an unspoken way, to begin the analysis by conducting myself in the initial meetings in a way that provides the patient a sense of what it means to be in analysis (Ogden 1989b). In the opening moments of the first meeting I may say nothing or may ask the patient, "Where should we begin?" My effort is to introduce the patient in the initial meeting (and in every subsequent meeting) to the nature of an analytic dialogue (which is characterized by a combination of qualities that the analysand will not have encountered elsewhere since the analytic dialogue is different from every other form of human discourse). I attempt to do this in a way that does not announce itself as a "technique" (i.e., as a stagnant, prescribed form). The "fundamental rule" in current analytic practice is in danger of becoming a frozen injunction for both analyst and analysand. It is often treated as a static, unexamined fixture in the analytic landscape carrying all the stifling power of Freud's (1913) repeated use of the words "must" and "insist" in his description of the introduction of the analysand to the fundamental rule.

It seems to me antithetical to the effort to generate an analytic process to exhort the patient to say everything that comes to mind. To do so would run counter to my conception of the analytic experience as being grounded in the dialectical interplay of the capacities of analyst and analysand for reverie (Ogden 1994a, d). It is as important for a patient to know that he is free to be silent as it is for him to know that he is free to speak. To privilege speaking over silence, disclosure over privacy, communicating over not communicating, seems as unanalytic as it would be to privilege the positive transference over the negative transference, gratitude over envy, love over hate, the depressive mode of generating experience over the paranoid-schizoid and autistic-contiguous modes of generating experience (Ogden 1986, 1988b).

It is the point at which these dialectics (for example, the dialectical tension of love and hate, disclosure and privacy, communicating and not communicating) have collapsed in one "direction" or another (for example, when an overvaluation of disclosure has led to the equation of privacy and resistance) that the individual (or the analytic pair) has entered the realm of psychopathology. From this perspective, psychopathology involves a variety of forms of failure of the individual (or of the analytic pair) to come to life in the process of generating and preserving these dialectical tensions and instead becoming engaged in creating substitutes for the experience of aliveness, for example, in the form of perverse pleasure, manic excitement, as-if constructions, and so on. I believe that to begin or found the analytic enterprise on a stated (or unstated) ideal that embodies a collapse of the dialectical tension of communicating and not communicating in the direction of disclosure represents an invitation into a pathological relationship. The outcome is often the creation of a iatrogenic illness in which the capacity for reverie is paralyzed or driven into hiding, thus making it significantly less likely that a genuine analytic process will ever take place.

At this point, I would like to offer a brief clinical example of a collapse of the dialectic of privacy and communication that resulted in an experience of psychological deadness.

I was consulted by Dr. E. about an analysis he was conducting that had felt "stagnant" to him for several years. The analyst felt oppressed by the patient, Ms. J., although Dr. E. said that he quite liked her. The analyst told me that he often wished that he could decrease the frequency of sessions from five times per week to two or three times per week, or perhaps terminate the analysis altogether. In the course of the extended consultation, I asked Dr. E. to present process notes from several sessions including a detailed account of his counter-transference responses to the patient.

Dr. E. described the way in which the patient would fill the hours with apparently introspective talk that "seemed to go nowhere." He told me that he often struggled to fight off sleep. Dr. E. added that his description of the feeling of the analysis would be incomplete if he omitted the fact that there were times when he felt painfully self-conscious during the sessions with this patient. Dr. E. said that Ms. J. could be extremely cutting in her "always perceptive" critique of his taste in clothing, slight weight changes, deportment, office decoration, and so on. Such comments were offered apologetically by the patient and were often prefaced by such remarks as, "I'm afraid I'll offend you or hurt you if I tell you what I'm thinking."

In one of the few dreams reported by the analysand, she was in a public place needing to take a shower, but found that none of the stalls had shower curtains. There was a modest, unassuming door that looked like a bathroom door

which led to a lovely apartment decorated in the
patient's favorite colors, deep reds and browns.
Ms. J. said that she had no thoughts about the
dream. I wondered aloud with Dr. E. whether the
dream might have reflected a painful, and thus far
unspoken, feeling of lack of privacy in the transference-countertransference. The "modest" door led
to a living space (a space where the patient could
be alive in privacy). It was a place that reflected a
style of her own. I said that the deep red and
brown colors seemed to suggest that sexual aliveness was part of what was being imagined and
experienced by the patient in the dream, and perhaps wished for in the transference.

In the course of the discussion of this dream, I
asked Dr. E. whether he had told Ms. J. that it was
her task to say everything that came to mind. He
said that he had told this to the patient at the
beginning of the analysis (seven years earlier), but
that this instruction had not been mentioned since
then by either of them.

I raised the possibility with Dr. E. that his feelings of being painfully and intrusively seen and
exposed by Ms. J. may reflect something of the
patient's projected experience of being sadistically
robbed of her own inner world. It seemed possible
that this fantasied destructive plundering was
occurring because both the analyst and analysand
had subjugated themselves to an imagined author-
ity, the "fundamental rule" and all that it symbol-

ized for both Dr. E. and for the patient. (Of course, no single factor such as the analyst's instructing the patient to say everything that comes to mind, will determine the course of an analysis. In the case being discussed, the analyst's instructions regarding the fundamental rule were a manifestation of an evolving intersubjective construction in which analyst and analysand were ensnared.)

A thorough discussion of this aspect of the transference-countertransference occurred over the succeeding months of consultation. One element in this discussion involved Dr. E.'s telling me that he had taken the fundamental rule as a "given" in part because it had served as a major component of the context in which his own analysis had been conducted. Dr. E. recognized in his own non-self-reflectiveness about this aspect of the analytic interaction, an acting-out of his resentment about this aspect of his own experience in analysis and suspected (on the basis of further reveries occurring during the sessions with Ms. J.) that he was involved in a fantasied retaliatory reversal of roles in the current analysis.

Dr. E. eventually told the patient that recent events in the analysis had reminded him of Ms. J.'s dream about the public showers that lacked shower curtains. He connected this image in part to his having instructed her to say everything that came to mind. Dr. E. told the patient that he hoped that analyses that he conducted would result in changes in him as well as in the patient. One change that had occurred over the previous seven years was his feeling about asking a patient to say everything that comes to mind. Showers should have shower curtains and analyses should have a place for privacy. The patient was greatly relieved by Dr. E.'s comments. Later in the session, she said that it had meant a great deal to her that he had spoken to her with such candor. Dr. E. told me that he could not recall Ms. J.'s ever having expressed gratitude to him in so direct and moving a way.

Reconceiving the Fundamental Rule

If I were to put into words for myself my view of the analysand's role in relation to communicating and not communicating in the analytic setting, I suppose it would begin with the notion that communicating and privacy are each to be valued as dimensions of human experience, each creating and preserving the vitality, the "sense of real" (Winnicott 1963, p. 184) of the individual and of the analytic experience. Formulated as a brief statement to an analysand, it might take the following form: "I view our meetings as a time for you to say what you want to ay, when you want to say it, and for me to respond in my own way. At the same time, there must always be a place for privacy for both of us." This is a long, rather awkward statement, and I am not sure that I have ever said this in precisely this way to an analysand. The statement sounds stilted to me, I think in part because it is an imaginary comment devoid of the personal context of a specific human interaction. Nonetheless, it captures a good deal of what I often say to myself, and, when the occasion arises, what I talk about with the patient.[2]

It is not infrequent that the analysand will have either read about the "fundamental rule," or devised a version of it for himself (for example, on the basis of experience with parents who were felt to require him to "tell all") or "learned about" the fundamental rule through experience in one or more previous analyses. Under such circumstances, it has been essential for me to talk with the patient about *his* conception of the "rules of analysis" relating to free association, i.e., *his* rules concerning the relationship between what is said and what is left unsaid, between what *must* be made public and what "is allowed to" remain private. Several patients have told me that on the basis of their experiences in previous analyses, they had come to assume

---

2. This view of the role of the analysand overlaps brief comments made by Altman (1976) and Gill (personal communication reported by Epstein, 1976) concerning their own versions of the fundamental rule. Altman (1976) suggests speaking to the patient in a way that conveys to the analysand that the analysand is "entitled to say anything" (p. 59). Gill (personal communication reported by Epstein 1976) suggests saying to the analysand, "You may say whatever you wish (p. 54). These two statements overlap with my own thinking, although they place far less emphasis than I do on the centrality of the role of privacy in the analytic experience.

that all analyses would eventually evolve into two con-
versations, one spoken, one secret, because of the "rule
about saying everything." Eventually, in the course of
these discussions, I have clarified that my own conception of analysis does not require the analysand to
attempt to say everything that comes to mind. Both the
analysand and I must always be as free to communicate
with ourselves (both in the form of words and sensations) as we are free to communicate with one another.

It has not been my experience in analyses I have
conducted or supervised than an analytic space in
which privacy is valued as much as communication
leads to analytic impasses in which silence, for example,
comes to serve as an unanalyzable form of resistance.
When extended defensive silences have occurred, I
have found it to be important to acknowledge and
interpret both the patient's need for privacy and his
need to make a transference communication through
silence (Coltart 1991). (The transference communication that is made through silence is often a form of
transference as "total situation" [Joseph 1985].)

Over time in an analysis, the idea of the
analysand's saying only what he wants to say and holding privacy as "sacred" (Winnicott 1963) proves to be
more complicated than it first appears since the
analysand is of course not always clear about what it is
that he would like to say or even who "he" is. The
analysand finds that the first person singular is in fact
plural: there are many "I's." After all, the patient wants
to say certain things while "he" (another aspect of his

experience of himself) finds that "he" cannot bring himself to say these things that "he" wants to say. Moreover, there are things that he feels he would like to say, but does not know what they are. (See Ogden 1992a, b for a discussion of the dialectically constituted/decentered subject of psychoanalysis). It is an important development in an analysis when an analysand becomes able to differentiate and understand something of the relationship between different aspects of himself, for example, between his not wishing to say something (because he wants to "keep it to himself" for the time being) and his not feeling able to say something while hoping that the analyst will help him find a way to be able to put it into words. Such conflicts between different aspects of self experience often remain unrecognized, and therefore unanalyzable, when an analysis is conducted under the aegis of the analyst's statement of, and the patient's partially defensive use of, the fundamental rule. This type of impasse may take the form of the patient's unconscious fantasy that analysis requires the patient to submit to a type of "psychic evisceration." The unconscious object relations constituting this fantasy remain unanalyzable so long as the analyst is unselfreflectively imposing an actual experiential context that is governed by the expectation/demand that the analysand "say everything that comes to mind."

The Role of the Analyst and the Fundamental Rule

Freud (1923a) believed that the fundamental rule of free association has its counterpart in the analyst's effort to "surrender himself to his own unconscious mental activity, in a state of evenly suspended attention" (p. 239). The analyst attempts "to avoid so far as possible reflection and the construction of conscious expectations, [and attempts] not to try to fix anything that he heard particularly in his memory, and by these means to catch the drift of the patient's unconscious with his own unconscious" (p. 239). The analyst's "work of interpretation [is] not to be brought under strict rules and [leaves] a great deal of play to the physician's tact and skill" (p. 239). "Or, to put it purely in terms of technique: 'He [the analyst] should simply listen, and not bother about whether he is keeping anything in mind'" (1912, p. 112).

Freud's emphasis in describing the "work" of the analyst is not on the analyst's seeing or revealing everything (even to himself), but on creating conditions for a particular sort of receptivity and "play" of the mind. Freud asks the analyst to attempt to allow his own unconscious to enter into a resonance with the unconscious of the patient. The analyst in "simply listening," attempts *not* to "get a fix" (not to remember or understand too much) and instead "simply" to use his own state of unconscious receptivity to get a sense of, to "catch the drift" of, the patient's unconscious experience. It seems to me that the psychological state described here by Freud as "simply listening" is the same psychological state that Bion (1962a) refers to as "reverie," a state characterized by the absence of "memory and desire" (Bion 1967).

Although the analyst's state of unconscious receptivity to the unconscious of the analysand is described as the analyst's giving "equal notice" (Freud 1912, p. 112) to himself (i.e., as the counterpart of the demand made on the patient in the fundamental rule), the effort to enter into a state of "evenly suspended attention" (Freud 1912, p. 111) seems hardly to represent "equal notice" to the demand that the analysand say everything that comes to mind. If the "demand" made on the patient (or better, the role assigned to the patient), were genuinely complementary in nature to the role Freud envisioned for the analyst in the process of creating a state of evenly suspended attention, I believe that the analytic pair could more easily enter into a type of relatedness in which it is possible for both the analyst and the analysand to "catch the drift of," get a sense of, the "current" of the unconscious constructions being generated in the analysis. Under these conditions, analyst and analysand are each in a position to "turn his own unconscious like a receptive organ towards the transmitting unconscious" (Freud 1912, p. 115) of the other and toward the jointly, but asymmetrically, created unconscious constructions of "the analytic third."

5

Dream Associations

As in the discussion of the use of the couch and "the fundamental rule" in the previous chapter, I shall take as a starting point in thinking about the analysis of dreams the idea that analytic technique must serve the analytic process. I view the analytic process as centrally involving the interplay of conscious and unconscious states of "reverie" (Bion 1962a, b) of analyst and analysand leading to the creation of a third subject of analysis ("the intersubjective analytic third") (Ogden 1994a, d). Further, the role of analytic technique in safeguarding the privacy of analysand and analyst is held to be as critical to the facilitation of the analytic process as is the role of analytic technique in creating and preserving conditions for conscious and unconscious communication between analyst and analysand. From the perspective of this conception of the analytic process, I shall in this chapter reconsider aspects of analytic technique related to the analysis of dreams.

For almost a century, beginning with Freud's (1900) experience in the analysis of his own dreams, there has been general agreement among psychoanalysts that the analytic understanding of dreams presented in the course of an analysis must be shaped by the network of associations and linkages that the patient generates in response to his dreams (see for example, Altman 1975, Bonime 1962, Etchegoyen 1991, French and Fromm 1964, Garma 1966, Gray 1992, Rangell 1987, Segal 1991, and Sharpe 1937). Dreams, particularly the latent content of dreams, have been viewed as the patient's unconscious constructions and the role of the analyst has been likened to that of the skillful obstetrician delivering a baby as unobtrusively and non-invasively as he can (S. Lustman 1969, personal communication). The analyst must give the patient room to associate as freely as possible to his dream. In the absence of the patient's associations, the analyst is left in the position of interpreting only manifest dream content, thus engaging in a superficial (and probably largely inaccurate) form of interpretation (Altman 1975, Garma 1966, Greenson 1967, Sharpe 1937). Given the importance of the patient's associations to his dream, it is widely held that the analyst must not interfere with the patient's associative process by making "premature" interpretations based on his own associations to the dream. If the patient does not provide associations, the analyst's role comes to center on exploring the analysand's unconscious anxiety/resistance to providing the associational linkages needed to understand and interpret his dream (including its transference meaning) (Gray 1994).

The analyst's offering of an interpretation concerning a dream in the absence of the patient's associations (without exploring the patient's anxiety in relation to associating to the dream) would be considered by many, if not most analysts to be a form of "wild analysis." After all, the analyst under such circumstances is simply offering his own associations. If the analyst is to avoid engaging in "wild analysis," the patient's unconscious, and not that of the analyst, must be the focus of the analytic enterprise.

What I have thus far presented (in a highly schematic form) as the "generally held" view of the principles of technique of dream analysis, represents, for me, a fundamental and indispensable component of the understanding of the analysis of dreams. However, in recent years, it has seemed increasingly important to supplement this view with a perspective that places the analysis of dreams in the context of an understanding of the dream as an intersubjective analytic event. In what follows, I shall attempt to explore the implications of the idea that a dream dreamt in the course of an analysis represents a manifestation of the intersubjective analytic third. With this perspective in mind, I shall propose a revised view of aspects of the tecique of dream analysis.

From the vantage point of the concept of the inter-subjective analytic third, the question of dream analysis in general, and the handling of dream associations in particular, becomes an even more interesting and com-plex endeavor than had previously been generally appreciated.[1] One might well ask whether it is any longer self-evident that the patient's associations to his dream should be privileged in the way that they have been in the past in relation to the analyst's conscious responses to the dream. Do we mean the same thing that we did even a decade or two ago when we speak of the patient's dream as "his" dream? Perhaps, it is more accurate to think of the patient's dream as being gener-ated in the context of an analysis (with its own history) consisting of the interplay of the analyst, the analysand, and the analytic third, and therefore the dream is no longer to be considered simply "the patient's dream." In other words, does it any longer make sense to speak of the patient as the dreamer of his dream or are there always several analytic subjects (dreamers) in dialectical tension, each contributing to every analytic construc-tion, even to a psychic event as seemingly personal (i.e., seemingly a production of the workings of the individ-

---

1. Isakower (1938) and Lewin (1950) were pioneers in the exploration of the analyst's use of his own consciousness as an "analytic instrument" (Isakower 1963), particularly in relation to the use of this function for purposes of understanding ʟne uncon-scious meanings of the patient's dreams and other sleep-related phenomena.

ual unconscious mind) as a dream or a set of dream associations[2]?

From the perspective being developed in this and in previous publications (Ogden 1992a, b, 1994a, b, c), it could be said that when a patient enters analysis, he in a sense "loses his mind" (in the process of creating a mind of his own). In other words, the psychological space in which his thinking, feeling, bodily experience and dreaming occurs is no longer entirely coincident with his "own mind" as he had experienced it to that point in his life. From the initial analytic meeting onward, the analysand's personal psychological space (including his "dream space") and the analytic space become increasingly convergent and difficult to differentiate. As a patient enters analysis, the analysand's experience of his mind (the locus of his psychological life and to a certain extent "the place where he lives" [Winnicott 1971c] and dreams) increasingly becomes "located" (in a feeling sense) in the space between analyst and analysand

---

2. Grotstein (1979) and Sandler (1976) have discussed the interplay of multiple unconscious *intrapsychic* aspects of the personality system in the process of dreaming a dream and understanding it. However, they do not address the intersubjective dimension of dreaming that is the focus of the current discussion. Blechner (1995) has discussed the analyst's use of the patient's dreams for purposes of understanding his own unconscious anxieties which understandings are then used to facilitate understanding of the transference.

(Ogden 1992b). This is a "felt place" that is by no means restricted to the analyst's consulting room. It is a mind (more accurately, a psychesoma) that is in a sense the creation of two people, and yet is the mind/body of an individual. (In words borrowed from a poem by Robert Duncan [1960], it is a place "that is not mine, but is a made place/that is mine, it is so near to the heart.")

As analyst and analysand generate a third subject, the analysand's experience of dreaming is no longer adequately described as being generated in a mental space that is exclusively that of the analysand. A dream created in the course of analysis is a dream arising in "the analytic dream space" and might therefore be thought of as a dream of the analytic third. Once again, we must not insist on an answer to the question, "Is the dream the analysand's dream, the analyst's dream or the dream of the analytic third?" The three must be held in an unresolved tension with one another.

As an experience generated in the (intersubjective) analytic dream space, a dream dreamt in the course of an analysis could be conceived of as a "joint construction" (in the asymmetrical sense described in Chapters 2 and 4) arising from the interplay of the unconscious of the analyst and the unconscious of the analysand. Since the analyst's associations to the dream experience are drawn from experience in and of the analytic third, they are no less important a source of analytic meaning in relation to the dream than are the patient's associations[3].

In the following brief clinical vignette, I will attempt to convey something of an analytic experience in which a patient's dream was treated by the analytic pair as having been generated in the intersubjective analytic dream space.

Mr. G. was a rather schizoid man in his early 40's whom I had been seeing in analysis for almost eight years. The patient was extremely well read in a wide range of subjects including psychoanalysis. Mr. G. began a session in this period of the analysis by telling me that a dream had awoken him during the night. He had felt quite shaken for some time after waking up. In the dream, his mother was her current age (in her early 70's) and was pregnant. Both she and the patient's older sister were very matter of fact about it, behaving as if there were nothing

---

3. Just as the dreams of the analysand are generated in the context of the analytic dream space, the analyst's dreams should similarly be treated as sources of analytic meaning in relation to the leading transference-countertransference anxiety at a given juncture of an analysis (Peltz 1996, Whitman et al. 1969, Winnicott 1947, Zweibel 1985). I have found that this is of particular importance when the analyst's dream is recalled during the course of an analytic hour (whether or not the patient is represented in the manifest content of the dream). It is beyond the scope of this discussion to explore and clinically illustrate the analyst's use of his own dreams in the analysis of the transference-countertransference.

unusual about what was happening. Their behavior and demeanor were so bizarre that the situation felt unreal even in the dream. The patient's mother and sister were busily and excitedly making plans about day to day practicalities connected with the pregnancy and the upcoming birth. The patient felt stunned in the dream and angrily told his mother and sister that he couldn't believe what a stupid thing his mother had done and could even less fathom how the two of them could be happy about this thing. He told me that it was agonizingly frustrating in the dream not to be able to find words that had the slightest effect on his mother.

As Mr. G. was telling me his dream, it was evident how painfully isolated he was feeling in describing what I imagined was his current version of his experience of learning of his mother's pregnancy with his younger brother. The patient was fourteen months old when his brother was born and consequently was in fact speechless (an infant) at the time of his mother's pregnancy. I imagined that the mother's excitement about, and absorption in, the pregnancy, birth and infancy of the patient's brother added insult to injury to the patient's sense of outrage at the mother's "secret" alliance with the father in this completely unexpected event. They had not even consulted him about this important matter! I speculated to myself that Mr. G.'s father had been banished from the manifest content of the dream and had been replaced by his sister in order to diminish the narcissistic sting of the acknowledgment of generational difference and parental intercourse.

The patient seemed to be wearing his heart on his sleeve in the dream in a way that was highly uncharacteristic of this extremely controlled man who was very little able to experience his own feelings. However, the patient had in the course of the previous months of analysis begun for the first time to feel warmth for me and trust in me and had been able to speak about those feelings, albeit in an extremely tentative and oblique way. As Mr. G. recounted the dream, I experienced a number of thoughts and feelings including a sense of detachment (reflected in my "translating" the dream in my mind into early developmental and abstract theoretical terms [e.g., "generational difference"]) as well as a mild sense of boredom. I also felt disappointed in myself for not being able to be more touched by a dream that was clearly very significant to Mr. G. and a novel experience for him (in the sense of revealing, in a rather undisguised way, intense, child-like feelings of anger, exclusion, and helplessness). The thought occurred to me that perhaps I had been doing analytic work for too long and was becoming jaded. I rather obsessionally added up in my mind the years I had been in practice in various places and became aware that I had been practicing in my current office for more than fifteen years. I looked around my consulting room and was struck by the heaviness of its contents—the ponderous Victorian moldings (the details of which I had perused for years), the singularly unimaginative mantle piece, the large wooden shutters with the slats glued into place by too many coats of paint. The idea of moving offices had crossed my mind many times over the years, but the thought of it at that moment left me feeling physically exhausted.

Mr. G. had told me on several occasions that he had felt sorry for his brother whom he felt had never been given a place in the family. However, it was only on experiencing my own indifference to "the best" that Mr. G. had to offer me (in his perfect specimen of an emotionally intense Oedipal dream) that I felt the full impact of what it was that Mr. G. had been so vehemently, speechlessly, impotently and futilely protesting in the dream. His protest was not simply the protest of an older sibling rebelling against the idea of having to share his mother with a new baby or against the idea that he was a baby produced by the sexual union and mature emotional and sexual alliance of his parents from which he was excluded and had no voice. What now seemed alive and immediate to me was Mr. G.'s protest against his mother's and my own indifference to his attempts at combating the way in which she/I felt lifeless, wooden, dense, immobile in our way of going through the motions of being a mother/analyst.

I said to Mr. G. that his description of his inability to make himself heard in the dream made me wonder if he had felt that I had seemed dense to him today or in recent meetings. (If I had had a more specific sense of, or even a speculation about what the patient might have been responding to, I would have included it in my comment.)

Mr. G. said without a pause, "Nothing has happened out of the ordinary. You've seemed the same as always to me." I said that while he apparently valued my steadiness, he seemed also to be suggesting with his words, "same as always," that he felt that there was something stagnant about what was going on between us. Mr. G. said that although he had not planned to talk to me about this until he returned (from his week-long summer holiday that was to begin in ten days), he was thinking about terminating the analysis at the end of the year. I had the strong impulse to muster an argument (disguised as an interpretation) designed to dissuade him from following through with this idea/plan about which I was being given no voice. It occurred to me that it was Mr. G. who was pregnant with the secret of the unwanted analysis while I had become the voiceless child. However, this idea seemed formulaic to me and had the effect of obscuring a feeling of embarrassment connected with my impulse to offer a pseudo-interpretation in an effort to hold onto Mr. G. The fantasied plaintive pseudo-interpretation brought to mind a conversation that I had had earlier in the week with a contractor whom I had known for many years and whom I considered a friend. In that

encounter with the contractor-friend, I had felt
unable to understand his state of mind. Over a
period of weeks he had repeatedly failed to make
good on promises that he had made to me about
work to be done. I had the odd feeling that his
words were disconnected from anything outside of
themselves and as a result I began to wonder if I
knew who he was. As I ruminatively went over our
recent conversation in my mind, I became increasingly anxious.

My awareness of the feelings in this reverie led
me to suspect that Mr. G. was afraid of losing the
connection that he had begun to feel with me and
feared that everything would be different between
us when he returned. It now seemed to me that
Mr. G. was attempting to protect himself against
such a surprise (and the awareness of his fears) by
preparing himself in his mind to leave me (while
projecting his helplessness into me).

I said to Mr. G. that I had the growing sense in
listening to him today that he was anxious that
something would happen while he was away that
would result in his returning to a person he didn't
know. I told him I wondered if he were worried
that on his return I would feel as unreal to him as
his mother had in the dream. (I was thinking of his
mother's inauthentic attempts to listen to him
[reflected in his feelings of unrealness in the
dream], as well as my fantasied pseudo-interpretation and my anxiety associated with my doubts and

uncertainty concerning the realness of the friendship with the contractor in my reverie.)

Mr. G. was silent for about a minute and then
told me that what I had said felt right. He added
that he felt both ashamed to be so childish and
glad that I knew him as well as I seemed to. There
was both warmth and distance in his voice. I was
struck by the way in which Mr. G., in the very act
of telling me that he appreciated the fact that I
understood him, was also conveying (with his
words "seemed to") his continued anxiety that I
would turn out to be a different person from the
one I appear to be. In the course of the succeeding meetings prior to the patient's vacation, it was
possible for Mr. G. and me to further discuss his
fear that the closeness that he had begun to experience with me would disappear without a trace
while he was away and that he would return to an
analyst whom he did not know and who did not
know him.

In this brief clinical account, I have attempted to
provide a sense of the intersubjective movement that
took place in a piece of analytic work involving a dream
and associations to it. My reverie began with the
detached, abstract somewhat mechanical "translation"
of the patient's dream in my own mind, accompanied
by feelings of boredom. I was disappointed in myself
for feeling so detached from a dream that seemed passionate and novel for Mr. G. I do not think that it is pos-

sible to say in any meaningful way where Mr. G.'s
dream stopped and where my reveries began.

My initial associations were associations both to his
dream and to my reveries (which included thoughts
about the ponderousness of my office and my own physical "stuckness" and psychic immobility.) My associa-
tions/reveries formed an important part of the basis for
an interpretation concerning the patient's experience
of me as densely impervious to him. The interpretation
was made before Mr. G. offered formal associations of
his own, but it did not feel to me as if I were preempting
him or leading him in a direction that reflected my psychology as distinct from his. At the time that I made the
initial interpretation, I had only a vague sense of the
leading transference-countertransference anxiety. However, the very incomplete interpretation allowed the
patient to indirectly (unconsciously) tell me more about
his sense of my staleness: "You've seemed the same as
always to me." My not being completely deaf to the
anger in his comment about my being "the same as
always" allowed Mr. G. to tell me of his thoughts about
terminating the analysis at the end of the year. On the
basis of awareness of my embarrassment about a fan-
tasy/impulse to offer the patient a pseudo-interpretation (reflecting a wish to cling to the patient) and my
reverie involving anxiety about the authenticity of the
friendship with the contractor, I was able to provide a
fuller interpretation. In this interpretation I addressed
what I had come to understand as the leading unconscious transference-countertransference anxiety: the
patient's fear of his returning to find that the person

that he felt he knew to be me had disappeared and that someone else had taken my place who appeared to be me, but did not feel like me.

The clinical vignette just presented represents an effort to illustrate something not only about a way of working with dreams in analysis, but, as importantly, represents an attempt to convey a sense of the type of movement that constitutes the experience of aliveness in the analytic setting. The generative movement between dream and reverie, between reverie and interpretation, between interpretation and experience in (and of) the analytic third, are for me the heart of that which is unique to the feeling of aliveness of an analytic experience.

Some Thoughts on Facets of the Technique of Dream Analysis

On the basis of the perspective that I have been describing, I have become more inclined to offer an interpretation or ask a question in response to a dream presented by the analysand without "waiting"[4]

---

4. It is important to bear in mind the atemporal nature of dreams and dream associations (Freud 1897, 1915, 1920, 1923b). If the analyst is focused on the associational events following the patient's telling of the dream, he may lose sight of the way in which the patient may have already associated to the dream, for example, in the form of the patient's facial expression on seeing the analyst in the waiting room or in the form of physical sensations or bodily movements occurring during the telling of the dream (Boyer 1988).

for the patient's associations. I find that it is often difficult afterwards to reconstruct in my own mind
whether it was the patient or I who first responded to
the dream. However, I also find that I usually respond
in an unhurried way to a dream presented by the
patient, thus giving the patient time to offer comments of his own if he is so inclined. To consistently
fail to give the patient time to respond to his dream
without interference from the analyst may give rise to
a form of transference-countertransference enactment in which the patient "serves up dreams" to the
analyst who ingests and digests them and returns to
the patient a narcissistic invention of the analyst in the
form of an interpretation.

I have found in my own work and in the work of
therapists and analysts whose work I have supervised
that the potential for spontaneity and generative
thought in the analytic dialogue is significantly
enhanced when analyst and analysand are released
from (or more accurately, release themselves from and
release one another from) the practice of privileging
the patient's associations to his dreams, and instead
treat the dream as a psychological event that is being
generated in the intersubjective analytic dream space.
When a dream is viewed as a product of the analytic
dream space, analyst and analysand have the freedom
to be receptive to the unconscious drift of the analytic
third as reflected in their reveries, their experiences of
"simply listening."

Before concluding this portion of the discussion
of the relationship of dreams to the analytic third, I

would like to briefly comment on the importance of *not understanding* dreams. Dreaming (or "dream-life") is a specific form of human experience that cannot be translated into a linear, verbally symbolized narrative without losing touch with *the effect* created by the dream experience itself, the experience of dreaming as opposed to the meaning of the dream (see Khan 1976, Pontalis 1977). For this reason, it seems to me particularly apt that the reveries (of analyst and analysand) serve as a principal psychological (and psychosomatic) medium through which dream experience is processed in the analytic setting. In the reveries of analyst and analysand, unconscious receptivity that sometimes involves "feats of association" (Robert Frost, quoted by Pritchard 1991, p.9) might take place in relation to a dream as opposed to thought processes through which a dream is deconstructed, "translated" (Freud 1913), understood or even interpreted. "Dreaming itself is beyond interpretation" (Khan 1976, p.47). In utilizing reverie as a principal form or shape in which dream experience is "carried" in the analytic setting, the analyst and analysand allow primary process, the "drift" of the unconscious (as opposed to its decoded message), to serve as a medium in which dream-life is experienced in the analytic space and an important component of the context in which dream analysis is conducted.

Concluding Comments

To return to the beginning, as one inevitably does in analytic thinking and practice: *analytic technique must serve the analytic process.* I view the analytic process as centrally involving a dialectical interplay of states of reverie of analyst and analysand resulting in the creation of a third analytic subject. It is through the (asymmetrical) experiencing of the analytic third by analyst and analysand that "the drift" of the unconscious internal object world of the analysand is understood and (eventually) verbally symbolized. The state of reverie of the analytic pair that is so critical a medium for the creation and experiencing of the analytic third requires conditions of privacy which must be safeguarded by analytic technique. The role of analytic technique in safeguarding the privacy of analysand and analyst is held to be as critical to the facilitation of the analytic process as is the role of analytic technique in creating and preserving conditions for conscious and unconscious communication between analyst and analysand. From the point of view of this understanding of the analytic process, I have attempted in this and the previous chapter to reconceive aspects of analytic technique and practice relating to the use of the couch, the "fundamental rule," and the analysis of dreams.

—— *6* ——
Reverie and Interpretation

Experience is never limited, and it is never
complete; it is an immense sensibility, a kind of
huge spider-web of the finest silken threads
suspended in the chamber of consciousness, and
catching every air-borne particle in its tissue. It is
the very atmosphere of the mind; and when the
mind is imaginative . . . it takes to itself the faintest
hints of life . . .

Henry James, 1884

I believe that we do well in psychoanalysis to allow
words and ideas a certain slippage. This is particularly
true of the term *reverie* (Bion 1962a, b). What I shall
attempt in this chapter is not a definition of reverie,
but a discussion of my own experience of attempting to
make use of my own states of reverie to further the ana-

lytic process. In this way I hope to convey a sense of what I mean by the experience of reverie in an analytic setting and how I make analytic use of the "overlapping states of reverie" of analyst and analysand.

It is almost impossible not to be dismissive of reverie since it is an experience that takes the most mundane and yet most personal of shapes. These shapes, especially early on in the process of moving toward verbal symbolization of reverie experience (and we are most of the time early on in the process), are the stuff of ordinary life—the day-to-day concerns that accrue in the process of being alive as a human being. Reveries "are things made out of lives and the world that the lives inhabit . . . [they are about] people: people working, thinking about things, falling in love, taking naps . . . [about] the habit of the world, its strange ordinariness, its ordinary strangeness . . . (Jarrell 1953, p. 68, speaking about Frost's poetry). They are our ruminations, daydreams, fantasies, bodily sensations, fleeting perceptions, images emerging from states of half-sleep (Frayn 1987), tunes (Boyer 1992) and phrases (Flannery 1979) that run through our minds, and so on.

I view reverie as simultaneously a personal/private event and an intersubjective one. As is the case with other highly personal emotional experiences of the analyst, he does not often speak with the analysand directly about his experiences, but attempts to speak to the analysand *from* what he is thinking and feeling. That is, he attempts to inform what he says by his awareness of and groundedness in his emotional experience with the patient.

It is no small thing that we ask of ourselves as analysts in attempting to make use of our reverie experience in the analytic setting. Reverie is an exquisitely private dimension of experience involving the most embarrassingly quotidian (and yet all important) aspects of our lives. The thoughts and feelings constituting reverie are rarely discussed with our colleagues. To attempt to hold such thoughts, feelings, and sensations in consciousness is to forego a type of privacy that we ordinarily unconsciously rely on as a barrier separating inside from outside, public from private. In our efforts to make analytic use of our reveries, "I" as unselfconscious subject is transformed into "me" as object of analytic scrutiny.

Paradoxically, as personal and private as the analyst's reveries feel to him, it is misleading to view the analyst's reveries as "his" personal creations since reverie is at the same time a jointly (but asymmetrically) created unconscious intersubjective construction that I have termed "the intersubjective analytic third" (Ogden 1994 a, b, c, d). In conceptualizing reverie as both an individual psychic event and an unconscious intersubjective construction, I am relying on a dialectical conception of the analytic interaction. The analyst and analysand together contribute to and participate in an unconscious intersubjectivity. Paraphrasing and extending Winnicott (1960), there is no such thing as an analysand apart from the analyst; at the same time the analyst and analysand are separate individuals, each with his own mind, body, history, and so on. The paradox is "to be accepted and tolerated and respected . . . for it us not to be resolved" (Winnicott 1971d, p.xii).

The analyst's reveries are in a way more difficult to make use of analytically than the dreams of either analyst or analysand because reveries are "unframed" by sleep and wakefulness. We can usually differentiate a dream from other psychic events because the experience occurs between the time we fall asleep and the time we wake up. Reverie, on the other hand, seamlessly melts into other psychic states. It does not have a clearly delineated point of departure or point of termination separating it, for example, from more focused secondary process thought that may precede or follow it.

The experience of reverie is rarely, if ever, "translatable" in a one-to-one fashion into an understanding of what is going on in the analytic relationship. The attempt to make immediate interpretive use of the affective or ideational content of the analyst's reveries usually leads to superficial interpretations in which manifest content is treated as interchangeable with latent content.

The analyst's use of his reveries requires tolerance of the experience of being adrift. The fact that the "current" of reverie is carrying the analyst anywhere that is of any value at all to the analytic process is usually a retrospective discovery and is almost always unanticipated. The state of being adrift cannot be rushed to closure. The analyst must be able to end a session with a sense that the analysis is at a pause, at best, a comma in a sentence. Analytic movement is better described as a "slouching towards" (Coltart 1986, borrowing from Yeats) rather than an "arriving at." This sort of movement is particularly important to be able to bear in one's handling of reverie. No single reverie or group of reveries should be overvalued by viewing the experience as a "royal road" to the leading unconscious transference-countertransference anxiety. Reveries must be allowed to accrue meaning without analyst or analysand feeling pressured to make immediate use of them. However urgent the situation may feel, it is important that the analytic pair (at least to some degree) maintain a sense that they have "time to waste," that there is no need to account for the "value" of each session, each week or each month that they may spend together. Symbolization (in part verbal) usually develops over time if one is patient and does not force it (cf. Green 1987 and Lebovici 1987, for discussions of the relationship between reverie and verbal symbolization). Forced symbolization is almost always easily recognizable by its intellectualized, formulaic, contrived quality.

Neither should any reverie be dismissed as simply the analyst's "own stuff," i.e., as a reflection of his own unresolved conflicts, his distress regarding events in his current life (however real and important those events might be), his state of fatigue, his tendency to be self-absorbed, and so on. An important event in the analyst's life, such as the chronic illness of his child, is differently contextualized by the analyst's experience with each patient, and as a result becomes a different "analytic object" (Bion 1962a, Green 1975) in each analysis. For example, while sitting with one patient the analyst may be consumed by the aspect of his experience involving his feelings of intense helplessness regarding his inability to relieve the pain that his child is experiencing. While with another patient (or at a different moment in the hour with the same patient), the analyst may be almost entirely preoccupied with feelings of envy of friends whose children are healthy. While with still another patient, the analyst might be filled with terrible sadness in imagining what it would feel like attempting to live without one's child.

The emotional fallout or wake of reverie is usually quite unobtrusive and inarticulate, carrying for the analyst more the quality of an elusive sense of being unsettled than a sense of having arrived at an understanding. I believe that the emotional disequilibrium generated by reverie is one of the most important elements of experience at the analyst's disposal with which to get a sense of what is happening at an unconscious level in the analytic relationship. Reverie is an emotional compass that I heavily rely on (but cannot clearly read) to gain my bearings in the analytic situation. Paradoxically, while reverie is for me critical to my ability to be an analyst, it is at the same time the dimension of the analytic experience that feels in the moment least worthy of analytic scrutiny. The emotional tumult associated with reverie usually feels as if it is primarily, if not entirely, a reflection of the way in which one is *not* being an analyst at that moment. It is the dimension of the analyst's experience that most feels like a manifestation of his failure to be receptive, understanding, compassionate, observant, attentive, diligent, intelligent, and so on. Instead, the emotional disturbances associated with reverie regularly feel to the analyst to be a product of his own interfering current preoccupations, excessive narcissistic self-absorption, immaturity, inexperience, fatigue, inadequate training, unresolved emotional conflicts, and so on. The analyst's difficulty in making use of his reveries in the service of analysis is easily understandable since such experience is usually so close, so immediate, that it is difficult to see: it is "too present to imagine" (Frost 1942a, p. 305).

Since I view the use of overlapping states of reverie of analyst and analysand as a fundamental part of analytic technique, a close examination of any analytic session or series of sessions will serve to illustrate significant aspects of the analytic use of reverie (or the difficulty faced by the analytic pair in attempting to do so). By the same token, a close examination of any given experience in the analytic use of reverie is specific to a particular moment in a particular analysis. An exploration of that moment will necessarily involve problems of technique and potentialities for emotional growth that are unique to that moment in the psychological-interpersonal movement of analyst and analysand. Consequently, the clinical example that I will present in an effort to illustrate the attempt to uti-

lize reverie experience in the analytic setting is necessarily a clinical example of a "special problem" in the
analytic use of reverie. (There are no "run of the mill"
problems in the effort to make use of reverie.)

Clinical Illustration:
The Woman Who Couldn't Consider

The following is a fragment of an analysis that focuses
on a series of three consecutive sessions that occurred
at the beginning of the sixth year of an analysis conducted five times per week.

> My stomach muscles tensed and I experienced a
> faint sense of nausea as I heard the rapid footfalls
> of Ms. B. racing up the stairs leading to my office.
> It seemed to me that she was desperate not to miss
> a second of her session. I had felt for some time
> that the quantity of minutes that she spent with me
> had had to substitute for all of the ways in which
> she felt unable to be present while with me. Sec-
> onds later, I imagined the patient waiting in a state
> of chafing urgency to get to me. As the patient led
> the way from the waiting room into the consulting
> room, I could feel in my body the patient's drink-
> ing in of every detail of the hallway. I noticed sev-
> eral small flecks of paper from my writing pad on
> the carpet. I *knew* that the patient was taking them
> in and hoarding them "inside" of her to silently
> dissect mentally during and after the session. I felt

in a very concrete way that those bits of paper were parts of me that were being taken hostage. (The "fantasies" that I am describing were at this point almost entirely physical sensations as opposed to verbal narratives.)

As Ms. B., a 41-year-old, divorced architect, laid down on the couch, she arched her back indicating in an unspoken way that the couch made her back ache. (She had in the course of the previous months complained on several occasions that my couch caused discomfort to her back.) I said to her that she seemed to be beginning the hour by registering a protest about the fact that it felt to her that I did not care enough about her to provide a comfortable place for her here. (Even as I was speaking these words, I could hear both the chilliness in my voice and the reflexive, canned nature of the interpretation. This was an accusation disguised as an interpretation—I was unintentionally telling Ms. B. about my own growing frustration, anger, and feelings of inadequacy in relation to our work together.)

Ms. B. responded to my comment by saying that that "is the way the couch is." (There was a hardness to the fact that the patient said "is" rather than "feels.")

The patient's bitter resignation to the fact that things are the way they are brought to mind the patient's conviction (which she treated as a fact) that she had been an unwanted baby, "a mistake," born almost a decade after her older brother and sister. Ms. B.'s mother had been advancing quickly in her career in the federal government when she became pregnant with the patient and grudgingly took a leave of absence for the first few months of the patient's life. Ms. B. felt that her mother had hated her all her life and had treated her from the beginning with a mixture of neglect and disgust while at the same time fiercely insisting that the patient be a "miniature version" of the mother. The patient's father, a shadowy figure in the analysis, was also part of the unchangeable "given" to which the patient felt resigned. He was described as a benign, but ineffectual man who seemed to have emotionally withdrawn from the family by the time the patient was born.

I said to Ms. B., in carefully measured tones, that she must feel that she perennially accommodates to me—I must seem to her not to have the slightest intention of accommodating to her. Both the patient and I knew that what we were talking about was a major struggle in the transference-countertransference: the patient's intense anger at me for not giving her what she *knew* I could easily give her if I chose to—a magically transformative part of me that would change her life. This was familiar territory and had been acted out in innumerable ways including, most recently, in the form of sexual activity involving her performing fellatio on a friend and triumphantly swallowing his semen, consciously fantasied to be his strength and vitality. I suspected that unconsciously Ms. B. fantasied the semen to be the magically transformative milk/power stolen from her mother and from me. The patient's attempts to steal a magically transformative part of me engendered in me a feeling that it was impossible to give her anything in the way of compassion or concern, much less affection or love, without feeling that I had submitted to her and was passively going through the motions of a role scripted by her.

Ms. B. then spoke about events that had occurred earlier in the day involving a long-standing dispute with a neighbor regarding a dog whose barking the patient found "unnerving." I recognized (with only a touch of amusement) that I was identifying with the neighbor's dog, who, it seemed to me, was being asked to be an imaginary dog (a dog invented by Ms. B.) who did not make the noises dogs do. Despite the fact that there seemed to be something about the transference displacement onto the neighbor's dog that I might have interpreted, I decided not to attempt such an intervention. I had learned from my experience with Ms. B. that a good deal of the effect being created by her monologue about the dog was the unstated demand the I point out to her something that she was already fully aware of (i.e., that when she was talking about the dog, she was also talking about me.) For me to do so, I imagined, would be experienced by the patient as a momentary victory in her effort to get me to "sting" her with an interpretation that reflected my anger/interest in her. She would in fantasy passively and gleefully swallow the stolen (angry) part of me. My experience with Ms. B. had also taught me that my succumbing to the pressure to make the demanding "stinging" interpretation was disappointing to the patient in that it reflected an inability on my part to hold onto my own mind (as she had found almost impossible to do while with her mother.) I also conceived of the patient's effort to evoke an angry response from me as an unconscious attempt to bring me (in the paternal transference) out of the shadows and into life. This too had many times been interpreted.

On the other hand, I could expect that if I were not to make an interpretation, Ms. B. would become increasingly withdrawn and move to another topic that would feel even more devoid of life than the session currently felt. The patient in the past, under such circumstances, had become somnolent in a way that was experienced by both of us as angrily controlling and at times she had fallen asleep for periods of up to fifteen minutes. When I interpreted the patient's withdrawal into sleep as a way of protecting herself and me from her anger (and mine), my experience had been that the patient would treat my words as precious commodities to be hoarded (like the scraps of paper on the carpet), rather than using them to generate her own ideas, feelings, responses, and so on. Similarly, interpretation of the patient's "use" of my interventions in this way had not been productive. Earlier discussions with Ms. B. concerning this form of analytic stalemate had led Ms. B. to quip that Oliver Sacks should write a story about her and call it "The Woman Who Couldn't Consider."

As Ms. B. was speaking and as I was mulling over the dilemma just discussed, I began thinking about a scene from a film that I had seen the previous weekend. A corrupt official had been ordered by his Mafia boss to kill himself. The corrupt official parked his car on the shoulder of a busy highway and put a pistol to the side of his head. The car was then filmed from a distance across the highway. The driver's side window in an instant became a sheet of solid red, but did not shatter. The sound of the suicide was not the sound of a gunshot, but the sound of uninterrupted traffic. (These thoughts were quite unobtrusive and occupied only a few seconds of time.)

Ms. B. went on without a pause or transition to speak about a date that she had had the previous evening. She described the man by means of a collection of disjointed observations that were quite devoid of feeling—he was handsome, well-read, displayed anxious mannerisms, and so on. There was almost no indication of what it had felt like for the patient to have spent an evening with him. I was aware that although Ms. B. was talking, she was not talking to me. It may have been that she was not even talking to herself in that it did not seem to me that she was the least bit interested in what she was saying. I had many times interpreted this sense of the patient's disconnection from me and from herself. I decided not to offer that observation as an interpretation here in part because I felt that it would have been experienced and utilized as another "sting" and I did not feel that I had a different way of talking to her.

As the patient continued, I was feeling that the hour was moving extremely slowly. I had the claustrophobic experience of checking the time on the clock and then some time later looking at the clock to find that the hands seemed not to have moved. Also, I found myself playing a game (which did not feel at all playful) of watching the second hand on the clock across the room make its silent rounds and finding the precise place in its movement that the digital clock on my answering machine next to my chair would transform one digit to the next. The convergence of the two events (the location of the second hand of the clock and the moment of the melting of the digital number on the answering machine) held my attention in a way that was oddly mesmerizing, although not exciting or fascinating. This was an activity that I had not previously engaged in during sessions with Ms. B. or with any other patient. I had the thought that this mental game may have reflected the fact that I was experiencing the inter-action with Ms. B. as mechanical, but this idea seemed rote and wholly inadequate to the disturb-ing nature of the claustrophobia and other poorly defined feelings that I was experiencing.

I then began (without being fully aware of it) to think about a phone call that I had received sev-eral hours earlier from a friend who had just had a diagnostic cardiac catheterization. He told me that emergency bypass surgery would have to be per-formed the next day. My thoughts and feelings moved from anxiety and distress about the friend's illness and imminent surgery to imagining myself being told the news that I required emergency bypass surgery. In the fantasy of my being given this news, I initially felt intense fear of never wak-ing up again from the surgery. This fear gave way to a sense of psychic numbness, a feeling of detachment that felt something like the onset of emotional dulling after rapidly drinking a glass of wine. That numbness did not hold and quietly slid into a different feeling that did not yet have words or images associated with it. The experiencing of this next feeling preceded any form of thought or image in a way that one sometimes awakes from sleep with intense anxiety, physical pain or some other feeling, and only several seconds later remembers the events in one's life or the dream with which the feelings are connected. In the instance I am describing in the session with Ms. B., I realized that the new feeling was one of profound loneliness and loss that was unmistakably connected with the recent death of a close friend, J. I recalled the feelings I had felt while talking with J. shortly after she had been diagnosed with a recurrence of her breast cancer. During a long walk on a weekend morning, we were both "figuring out" what the next step should be in the treatment of her then widely metastasized cancer. There was during that walk (I think for both of us) a momentary respite from the full intensity of the horror of what was occurring as we weighed alternatives as if the cancer could be cured. As I went over parts of the conversation in my mind, it seemed in retrospect that the more practical we became the more make-believe the conversation felt—we were creating a world together, a world in which things worked and had cause and effect relationships with one another. It was not an empty sense of make-believe, but a loving one. After all, it is only fair that 3 plus 8 equals 11. Embedded in this part of the reverie was not only a wish for fairness, but a wish for someone to enforce the rules. At that point in the flow of reverie, I became aware in a way that I had not previously experienced that the make-believe world that J. and I had been creating was a world in which there was no such thing as "we": she was dying, I was talking about *her* dying. She had been alone in it in a way and to a degree that I had never dared feel before that moment in the session. I felt a very painful sense of shame about the cowardice that I felt I had displayed in having protected myself in the way that I had. More importantly, I felt that I had left J. even more isolated than she had had to be by not fully recognizing the extent of her isolation.

I then refocused my attention on Ms. B. She was speaking in a rather pressured way (with an exaggerated lilt in her voice) about the great pleasure that she was deriving from her work and from the feeling of mutual respect and friendly collaboration that she experienced with her colleagues in her architectural firm. It seemed to me that only thinly disguised by the idealized picture being presented were feelings of loneliness and hopelessness about the prospect of her ever genuinely experiencing such feelings of ease and closeness with her colleagues, her friends, or me.

As I listened to Ms. B.'s pressured description, I was aware of feeling a combination of anxiety and despondency, the nature of which was quite nonspecific. I was reminded of the grim satisfaction that I had felt earlier in tracking the convergence of the precise, repeatable location of the sweep second hand of the clock and the instant of movement of the digital numbers on the answering machine. I thought that perhaps the fact that there was a place and a moment where the second hand and the digital clock "squared" may have rep-

resented an unconscious effort on my part to create a feeling that things could be named, known,
identified, located, in a way that I knew that they
could not.

Ms. B. began the following session with a
dream:

> I was watching a man take care of a baby in an
> outdoor place of some sort that might have
> been a park. He seemed to be doing a good
> job of attending to it. He carried the baby
> over to a steep set of concrete stairs and lifted
> the baby as if there were a slide to place it on,
> but there was no slide. He let go of the baby
> and let it hurdle down the stairs. I could see
> the baby's neck break as it hit the top step and
> I noticed that its head became floppy. When
> the baby landed at the bottom of the steps,
> the man picked up its motionless body. I was
> surprised that the baby was not crying. It
> looked directly into my eyes and smiled in an
> eerie way.

Although Ms. B. often began her sessions
with a dream, this dream was unusual in that it
was disturbing to me. This led me to feel a flicker
of hopefulness. The patient's dreams in the past
had felt flat and did not seem to invite inquiry or
discussion. Ms. B. made no mention of the dream
and immediately began to talk in an elaborately

detailed way about a project at work with which she had been involved for some time. I interrupted her after several minutes and said that I thought that in telling me the dream she had attempted to say something to me that she felt was important that I hear and at the same time she was afraid to have me hear it. Her burying the dream in the noise of the details of the project made it appear that she had said nothing of significance to me.

Ms. B. then said, in an earnest, but somewhat compliant way, that as she was telling me the dream, she at first felt identified with the baby in that she often feels dropped by me. She quickly and unexpectedly went on to say that this interpretation felt to her like a "kind of a lie" since it felt like a "tired old refrain, a knee-jerk reaction."

The patient then said that there were several very upsetting things in the dream beginning with the fact that she had felt "immobilized" and unable to prevent from happening what she saw unfolding. (I was reminded of the shame that I had felt in the previous session in connection with the thought that I had shielded myself from J.'s isolation and in a sense had looked on in an immobilized manner.) Ms. B. said that even more distressing to her was her sense of herself as both the baby and the man in the dream. She recognized herself in the baby's act of pointedly looking into her eyes and smiling in a detached, mocking way.

Ms. B. said that the baby's smile felt like the invisible smile of triumph that she often inwardly gives me at the end of each meeting (and at various junctures during the meetings) indicating that she is "above" or "immune to" psychological pain and that this makes her much more powerful than I am (despite what I may think).

I was moved by the patient's conscious and unconscious efforts to tell me, albeit indirectly, that she had some sense of what it had felt like for me to have had to endure her defiant claims not to need me and her triumphant demonstrations of her capacity to occupy a place above (outside of) human experience and psychological pain.

Ms. B. then told me that she was very frightened by how easy it is for her to become the man and the baby in the dream, that is, how easily she enters into a "robotic" mode in which she is fully capable of destroying the analysis and her life. She said that she was terrified by her capacity to deceive herself in the way that the man seemed to believe that he was placing the baby on a slide. Ms. B. told me she could easily destroy the analysis in this mindless way. She felt that she could not at all rely on her ability to distinguish real talk that is aimed at change from "pseudo-talk" that is designed to make me think she is saying something when she isn't. Ms. B. said that even at that moment she couldn't tell the difference between what she really felt and what she was inventing.

I will only schematically present elements of the subsequent meeting in an effort to convey a sense of the shape of the analytic process that was set in motion by the two sessions just described.

The next meeting began with Ms. B.'s picking a piece of loose thread from the couch and, in an exaggerated gesture of disdain, holding it in the air between her thumb and forefinger and dropping it on the floor before she laid down. When I asked her what it felt like to begin our meeting as she had, she laughed embarrassedly as if she were surprised by my inquiry. Sidestepping my question, she said that she had been in a compulsive cleaning frenzy from early that morning. She has awoken at 4:00 A.M. in a state of great agitation that seemed to be relieved only by cleaning her house, particularly the bathroom. She said that she felt that she had failed in life and in analysis and that there was nothing to do but to control "the ridiculous things" that she had it in her power to control. (I could feel her desperation, but her explanation seemed textbookish.) The patient went on to fill the first half of the session with ruminative thinking. My efforts to interpret the compulsive/ruminative activities as an anxious response to her having said too much (made a "mess") in the previous day's meeting were given only perfunctory notice before Ms. B. resumed her ruminations.

While the patient was in the throes of her defensive ruminations, I found myself watching the play of sunlight on the glass vases near one of the windows in my office. The curves of the vases were lovely. They seemed very feminine, resembling the curves of a woman's body. A bit later I had an image of a large stainless steel container in what seemed to be a factory, perhaps a food processing plant. My attention in the fantasy was anxiously riveted on the gears at the end of one of the containers. The machinery was clanking loudly. It was not clear what was frightening me, but it seemed that the gears were not working as they should and that a major malfunction with catastrophic results was about to occur. I was reminded of the extreme difficulty Ms. B. and her mother had had with breast-feeding. According to Ms. B.'s mother, the patient bit the mother's nipples so hard that they became inflamed and breast-feeding was terminated.

I had the thought that I was experiencing a sensuous and sexual aliveness with Ms. B., but had been made anxious by it and had turned her femininity (her breasts in particular) into something inhuman (the stainless steel container and its nipple/gears). It seemed that I was feeling that catastrophic breakdown would follow closely on the heels of sexual desire for, and sensual pleasure with, Ms. B. These desires and fears came as a surprise to me since to this point I had felt no sexual or sensual attraction to Ms. B., and in fact, had been aware of the aridity and boredom that had resulted from the stark absence of this dimension of experience. I thought of the way in which Ms. B. had arched her back two sessions earlier and for the first time experienced the image of her arching her back on the couch as an obscene caricature of sexual intercourse.

With about twenty minutes remaining in the session, Ms. B. said that she had come today wanting to tell me a dream that had awoken her during the night, but that she had forgotten it until that moment:

> I've just had a baby and I'm looking at it in the bassinet. I don't see anything of me in its face which is dark, heart-shaped, Mediterranean. I don't recognize it as something that came out of me. I think, "How could I have give birth to such a thing?" I pick it up and hold him, and hold him, and hold him and he becomes a little boy with wild curly hair.

Ms. B. then said, "In telling you the dream, I was thinking of the fact that what comes out of me here doesn't feel like me. I don't take any pride in it or feel any connection with it." (I was aware that the patient was leaving me out of the picture, a fact that was particularly striking given that my hair is curly. I was also struck by the aliveness of the dream in the hour and the way this seemed to be in part generated by the patient's

telling it in the present tense which was unusual
for her.)

I said to the patient that I thought that it
seemed true that she felt disgusted by everything
that came out of her here, but that I thought that
in telling me the dream she was saying something
more than that to me. I said she seemed quite
frightened of feeling or letting me feel the love she
felt for the child in the dream. I asked if she had
experienced the change of feeling when she
shifted from referring to the child as a "thing" or
"it" to using the word "him" when she said that she
had picked it up and held him and held him and
held him. Ms. B. fell silent for a minute or two during which time I had the thought that I may have
prematurely used the word "love" which was a
word that I could not at that moment remember
either of us ever having used during the entire
course of the analysis.

Ms. B. then said that she had noticed that
change in telling me the dream, but she could feel
it *as a feeling* only when she listened to me saying
her words. The patient told me that while I was
speaking, she felt grateful to me for my not letting
that part of things be "thrown away," but at the
same time she felt increasingly tense with each word
that I spoke for fear that I would say something
embarrassing to her. She added that it was as if I
might undress her and she would be naked on the
couch. After another silence of almost a minute,

Ms. B. said that it was hard to tell me this but the thought had gone through her mind as she was imagining being naked on the couch that I would look at her breasts and find them to be too small.

I thought of the agony surrounding J.'s surgery for breast cancer and became aware at this point in the hour that I was feeling both a wave of the deep love that I felt for J. together with the sadness of the enormous void that her death had left in my life. This range of feeling had not previously been part of my experience while with Ms. B.

[handwritten marginal note: "becomes free to feel" with "this patient"]

By this point in the hour, I found myself listening and responding to Ms. B. in quite a different way. It would be an overstatement to say that the feelings of anger and isolation had disappeared, but they were now part of a larger constellation of emotion. No longer was the isolation simply an encounter with something that felt non-human; rather, the isolation felt more like an experience of missing the humanness of Ms. B. that I viscerally knew to be there, but was only being allowed to fleetingly glimpse from afar.

I told the patient that I thought that her dream and our discussion of it also seemed to involve feelings of sadness that large parts of her life were being unnecessarily wasted, "thrown away." I said that she began telling me the dream by saying "I've just had a baby," but a great deal of what followed was about the ways in which she prevented herself from living the experience of hav-

ing a baby. (In the course of the analysis, Ms. B.
rarely had had fantasies or dreams of having a
baby and only twice that I could recall had discussed the question of whether she might ever
want to have children.) There were tears on her
face, but no sound of crying in her voice as she
said that she had not previously put the feeling
into words, but a good deal of her shame about
her breasts is that they feel like boys' breasts that
could never make milk for a baby.

Discussion

I began the presentation of the first of three sessions
occurring in the sixth year of Ms. B.'s analysis with a
description of my response to hearing the patient's
rapid footsteps on the stairs leading to my office. I find
it invaluable to be as fully aware as I can of what it feels
like to meet the patient each session (including the
feelings, thoughts, fantasies, and bodily sensations
experienced in anticipation of that particular meeting.) Much of my response to Ms. B. that day, both in
listening to her approach my office and in encountering her in the waiting room, was in the form of bodily
responses ("phantasies in the body" [Gaddini 1982]). I
was from the outset anticipating (in fantasy) being
physically and psychologically invaded by the patient:
my stomach muscles tensed as I unconsciously awaited
receiving a blow to the abdomen and I was experiencing nausea in preparation for evacuating a noxious

presence that I expected to experience inside of me. These feelings were elaborated in the form of fantasies of the patient's chafing to "get to me" (to get into my office/body) and fantasies of her cannibalizing me through her eyes as she took parts of me hostage in "drinking in" the scraps of paper from my notebook that she noticed on the carpet.

Clearly, this reverie, occurring even before the patient entered the consulting room, reflected a set of transference-countertransference feelings that had been growing in intensity and specificity for some time and yet were not available to either the patient or to me for reflective thought or verbal symbolization. This aspect of the analytic relationship was largely experienced by both of us as simply the way things were.

I experienced Ms. B.'s arching of her back only as a complaint and was not at that point able to entertain the possibility that the gesture had other meanings. My initial interpretation addressed the idea that the patient was angrily protesting my unwillingness to provide a comfortable place for her in my office. I could hear and feel the chilliness in my voice that transformed the interpretation into an accusation. I was at that moment feeling unable to be an analyst with the patient and instead was experiencing myself as angry, at sea, and rather helpless to alter the course of events. The "canned" nature of my interpretation alerted me to my own emotional fixity in relation to Ms. B. and to my inability at that point to think or to speak freshly or to render myself open to new possibilities for understanding and experiencing what was occurring between us. These realizations were deeply unsettling to me.

Although aspects of the patient's experience of her parents went through my mind at this point, I was very little able to bring that context to bear on the present situation in a way that felt real. Moreover, the constellation of ideas about the transference-counter-transference that had evolved in the course of this period of analysis (for example, the idea that the patient was relentlessly demanding magically transformative milk/semen/power) had lost most of the vitality that it once had held. At the juncture in analysis being described, these ideas had become for both the patient and for me stagnant formulae that largely served as a defense both against feelings of confusion and helplessness and against the experience of a fuller range of feelings (including loving ones).

Perhaps the disturbing awareness of the way my anger was interfering with my ability to offer utilizable interpretations allowed for the beginnings of a psychological shift to occur in me that was reflected in my ability to see (and feel) the humor involved in my identifying with the neighbor's dog who was (I felt) being asked not to be a dog and instead was being asked to be the patient's imaginary, invented creature. This led me to be able to refrain from offering still another intervention of the chilly, clenched teeth ("carefully measured") variety, and instead, to attempt to listen.

It was after this affective shift occurred that reverie of a more verbally symbolic (less exclusively somatic) sort began to be elaborated. The reverie that occurred at this point in the session consisted of a set of images and feelings (derived from a film) in which a corrupt official is ordered to commit suicide. He does so in such a way that the sound of the suicide is not that of rapid breathing, the report of a gun, the shattering of glass, or the spraying of blood, but the uninterrupted sound of traffic oblivious to this solitary human event. Although the images of this reverie were emotionally powerful, they were at this point so unobtrusive, so barely available to self-reflective consciousness that they served almost entirely as an invisible emotional background.

The experience of this reverie, although hardly noticed and not consciously utilized at the time it occurred, was nonetheless unsettling and contributed to the creation of a specific emotional context for the unconscious framing of what followed. Ms. B.'s account of her date the previous night was experienced differently than it would have been otherwise. The principal effect on me of her talk was the creation of a painful awareness of the feeling of not being spoken to, a sense of words filling empty space, words not spoken by anyone to anyone (even to herself).

Feeling at a loss to know how to speak to the patient about her not talking either to me or to herself, I continued to keep silent. Again I found my mind wandering, this time to a brief immersion in the mental "game" of observing the precise place and time of the convergence of movement of the digital time of the answering machine and the sweep second hand of the clock across the room. In part, this served to relieve the claustrophobia I was experiencing in feeling trapped *alone* with Ms. B. I hypothesized that both the reverie about the suicide and the "game" involving the workings of two time pieces may have reflected my sense of the mechanical, non-human qualities of the experience with Ms. B., but this idea seemed superficial and hackneyed.

The reveries that followed reflected a movement from a rather rigid, repetitive obsessional form to a far more affect-laden "stream of thought" (Wm. James 1890). I felt distressed in recalling a phone call from a friend who had been told he needed emergency open-heart surgery. Very quickly I protected myself from the fear of his dying by narcissistically transforming the event in fantasy into a story of my receiving this news. My own fear of dying was expressed as a fear of "never waking up." The idea of not waking up was at this juncture unconsciously overdetermined and in retrospect seems to have included both a reference to the oppressive "living death" of the analysand as well as to my own anaesthetized state in the analysis from which I unconsciously feared I would never awake.

In all of this there was a rapidly growing sense of being out of control both in relation to my own body (illness/sleep/death) and in relation to people I loved and depended upon. These feelings were momentarily allayed by a defensive withdrawal into emotional detachment, a psychic numbness. My unconscious efforts at emotional detachment did not hold for very long and gave way to a form of reverie in the shape of vivid images of a time spent with a very close friend, J., in the midst of her attempting to wrestle with imminent death. (I would only for want of a better word refer to the creation of these reverie images as "remembering" because the idea of remembering too strongly connotes something fixed in memory that is "called up to consciousness *again*" [remembered]. The experience in the session was not a repetition of anything, not a remembering of something that had already occurred; it was an experience occurring for the first time, an experience being generated freshly in the unconscious intersubjective context of the analysis.)

In the course of the reverie of the conversation with J. (in which make-believe, but desperately real efforts were being made to "figure out" what next to do), an important psychological shift occurred. What began in the reverie as a wishful insistence that things be fair and "make sense" became a painful feeling of shame regarding my sense that I had failed to appreciate the depth of isolation that J. was experiencing. The symbolic and affective content of the reverie was barely conscious and did not yet constitute a conscious self-awareness of isolation about which I could speak to myself or from which I could speak to the patient. Nonetheless, despite the fact that a conscious, verbally symbolized understanding of the reverie experience did not take place at this moment, an important *unconscious* psychological movement did occur which, as will be seen, significantly shaped the subsequent events of the hour.[1]

In "returning" the focus of my attention to Ms. B., I was not going back to a place I had been in the session, but was going to a new psychological "place" that had not previously existed, a place in part emotionally generated by the reverie experiences that I have just described. Ms. B. was speaking in an anxiously pressured, idealizing way about relationships with colleagues. The reverie experiences discussed above (including my experience of defensive psychic numbing) had left me acutely sensitive to the experience of psychological pain disguised by reliance on manic defense, particularly the pain of efforts to live with terrible loneliness and in isolation with one's feelings of powerlessness.

The "clock-game" reverie that had occurred earlier in the hour took on new meaning in the emotional

---

1. The unconscious movement brought about by the reverie experience might be thought of as the outcome of the unconscious "understanding work" (Sandler 1976) that is an integral part of dreaming (and reverie). Dreaming and reverie always involve an unconscious internal discourse between "the dreamer who dreams the dream and the dreamer who understands the dream" (Grotstein 1979). If there were no such unconscious discourse (if there were no unconscious "understanding work" standing in relation to the unconscious "dream work"), we would have to conclude that only the dreams (or reveries) that we remember have psychological value and contribute to psychological growth. This is a view to which few analysts would subscribe.

context of what was now taking place. The "earlier" reverie was in an important sense occurring for the first time in that the act of recalling it in the new psychological context made it a different "analytic object." The "mental game" as I experienced it at this point was filled not with boredom, detachment and claustrophobia, but with desperateness that felt like a plea. It was a plea for someone or something to rely on, some anchoring point that could be known and precisely located, that would, if only for a moment, stay put. These were feelings that in the hour felt "multi-valent," that is, they seemed simultaneously to have a bearing on my feelings in relation to J. and in relation to the evolving analytic relationship.

The affective movement just described is not accurately conceptualized as the "uncovering" of heretofore "hidden" feelings in relation to my own past experience with J. It would be equally misleading to reduce what was occurring in this regard to a process on which the patient was helping me to "work through" my previously unresolved unconscious conflicts in relation to J. (a process that Searles [1975] referred to as the patient's serving as "therapist to the analyst"). Rather, I conceive of the reverie experiences generated in the hour that I am describing as reflecting an unconscious intersubjective process in which aspects of my internal object world were elaborated in specific ways that were uniquely defined by the particular unconscious constructions being generated by the analytic pair. The emotional change that I experienced in relation to my (internal

object) relationship with J. could have taken place in
the way that it did only in the context of the specific
unconscious intersubjective relationship with Ms. B.
that existed at the moment in the analytic relationship
being described. The internal object relationship with J.
(or with any other internal object) is not a fixed entity;
it is a fluid set of thoughts, feelings, and sensations that
is continually in movement and is always susceptible to
being shaped and re-structured as it is *newly* experienced in the context of each new unconscious intersubjective relationship. In every instance it will be a
different facet of the complex movement of feeling constituting an internal object relationship that will be most
alive in the new unconscious intersubjective context. It
is this that makes each unconscious analytic interaction
unique both for analyst and analysand. I do not conceive of the analytic interaction in terms of the analyst's
bringing pre-existing sensitivities to the analytic relationship that are "called into play" (like keys on a piano
being struck) by the patient's projections or projective
identifications. Rather, I conceive of the analytic process as involving the creation of new unconscious intersubjective events that have never previously existed in
the affective life of either analyst or analysand.

Ms. B.'s experience of and participation in the
unconscious intersubjective movement that I have been
describing was reflected in the dream with which she
began the second of three sessions presented. In that
dream the patient was watching a man take care of a
baby. The man placed the baby on an imaginary slide

and allowed it to fall down a concrete staircase breaking its neck in the process. At the end of the dream, as the man picked up the silent, motionless baby, the infant looked directly into the patient's eyes and smiled eerily.

Ms. B. went on after reporting the dream as if she had not said anything of significance regarding her dream life or any other part of her life. I found (without planning it) that the wording of the interpretation I offered drew upon both the imagery of my reverie of the traffic noise covering the solitary suicide as well as the emotional effect on me of the absolute silence that framed the patient's dream (no spoken words, cries, screams, snaps, thuds occurred in Ms. B.'s account of the dream). I commented on the way the patient had used words as "noise" to talk over (drown out) something of great importance that she both hoped I would hear and was trying to prevent me from hearing in her telling me the dream. The question of where my reveries stopped and the patient's dream began was not possible to determine in any meaningful way at this point. Both my reveries and the patient's dream were created in the same "intersubjective analytic dream space" (see Chapter 5).

Ms. B's response to my interpretation was more direct, self-reflective, and affectively colored than had been the case for some time. Despite a note of compliance, it was clear that the analytic relationship was in the process of changing. After beginning by saying that she saw herself as the baby that was being dropped by me, the patient was able to observe that the interpreta-

tion was a "kind of a lie" in that it felt stale and reflexive. She then spoke of feeling "immobilized" in her
inability to prevent what she was observing from happening. My reverie from the previous session involving
my sense of shame associated with the feeling of being
an immobilized observer of J.'s isolation led me to wonder whether shame and guilt were important aspects of
the patient's distress in relation to the dream as well as
in relation to her treatment of me. Ms. B.'s next comments seemed to bear out this understanding: she told
me indirectly that she was frightened of her capacity to
isolate herself and me through her claims to be "above"
or "immune to" psychological pain.

As Ms. B. spoke about her use of the "eerie smile"
with me, I was not certain whether the patient was conscious of her efforts to relieve me of my feelings of isolation while with her. This session concluded with the
patient's speaking *to me* about her fear of her capacity
to become so invulnerably mechanical that she is capable of destroying the analysis and her life. In her experiencing in the moment her inability to distinguish real
feeling from deceptive "pseudo-talk," Ms. B., without
fully recognizing it, was talking to me about the only
things that she could know in any visceral way to be
real—her frightening awareness of not knowing what,
if anything, is real about her and the feeling of being
fully entrapped in herself.

The following meeting began with a theatrical acting-in in which Ms. B. fastidiously removed a piece of
loose thread from the couch. It had been a long-stand-

ing pattern for the patient to anxiously withdraw after sessions in which it had felt to me that we had spoken to one another in a way that reflected a feeling of human warmth. Nonetheless, the imperious, detached quality of the patient's gesture left me with a distinct feeling of disappointment that the connection I had begun to feel with Ms. B. had again abruptly been brought to an end. I felt that I was being dropped with about as much concern as she was feeling toward the piece of thread that was being dropped to the floor.

It seemed that she too was experiencing disappointment in herself, feeling herself to be a failure in life and in analysis. The patient was also apparently feeling frightened and embarrassed that she had (in fantasy) soiled herself and me and was feverishly engaged in cleaning up the spilled bodily contents/feelings (the dirty bathroom mess). My efforts to talk with Ms. B. about what I thought I understood about the way her current feelings and behavior represented a response to what she had experienced with me in the previous meeting were systematically ignored.

During the bulk of the session, while the patient was ruminating, my own reveries included a sensuous enjoyment of the feminine lines created by the play of sunlight on the vases in my office. These feelings were followed by an anxiety-filled set of reverie images of malfunctioning gears on containers in a factory that may have been a food processing plant. There was a strong sense of impending disaster. These images and feelings were connected in my mind with the patient's descrip-

he does not get caught in
olc. that... quite
Zen like

194   *Reverie and Interpretation*

tion of the very early termination of breast-feeding that had resulted from her "excessive" desire (her biting her mother's nipples so hard that they became inflamed).

It felt to me that despite the fact that I had not previously experienced any hint of sexual or sensual aliveness while with Ms. B., I was now beginning to feel these feelings and was in fact experiencing anxiety about the catastrophe that such feelings would in fantasy bring on. I was reminded of Ms. B.'s arching her back at the beginning of the session earlier in the week and recalled how the gesture had held no sexual force for me at the time. That bodily movement now seemed to me to be a denigrating caricature of sexual intercourse, that is, both an expression of sexual desire toward me and the simultaneous denigration of that desire.

The thoughts as well as the reverie feelings and images just described served as the emotional context for my listening and responding to the dream that the patient presented in the second half of the hour. In that dream, Ms. B. had just given birth to a baby that felt alien to her. On holding him and holding him and holding him, he turned into a little boy with wild curly hair. Ms. B. quite uncharacteristically offered her own interpretation of the dream saying that she felt that it reflected the way in which she feels no connection with what comes out of her in the analysis. I acknowledged that this did seem to capture something she had felt for a long time, but (influenced by the feeling residue of my reveries), I told her that I thought that she was telling me more than that in telling me the dream. I said that I thought that it was frightening to Ms. B. to openly experience affection for her child. (I chose to defer until a later session interpreting the idea/wish that the curly haired baby was "ours" because it seemed necessary that the patient first be able to genuinely experience her own connection with him [me/herself/the analysis.] I then asked if Ms. B. had felt the way in which, almost despite herself, she had allowed the baby to become human (and loved) as she moved mid-sentence from referring to the infant as "it" to using the word "him" in her saying, "I pick it up and hold him and hold him and hold him."

After a silence that felt both thoughtful and anxious, Ms. B. told me that she had felt grateful that I had not "thrown away that part of things." I was aware that Ms. B. was using vague language ("that part of things") instead of using the word "love" (as I had done), or introducing a word of her own to name the feeling that was "not thrown away." She went on to tell me that she had been afraid that I would embarrass her with my words (in fantasy, undress her) and that her breasts would be revealed and that I would find them to be too small.

I then experienced in a way that I had not been able to feel in the course of the analysis to that point the intensity of the love that I felt for J. as well as the depth of my feelings of sadness and loss. It was only at that juncture that I began to suspect that the feelings of shame that I had felt during the reverie about J. in the earlier session had served to protect me from experiencing the pain of that love and the feeling of loss. I suspected that Ms. B.'s shame regarding the fantasy of my finding her breasts too small similarly served as a defensive function in relation to the more frightening wishes to be able to love me and to feel loved by me (as well as the accompanying fears of my contempt for her and her contempt for herself for having such wishes). This fearful, defensive contempt had been expressed in her imperious gesture at the start of the meeting.

The reveries and thoughts that I have just described (for example, the reveries involving an anonymous suicide, the effort to control the passage of time, the inability to fully grieve the early death of a friend, the anxiety associated with foreclosed sexual and sensual aliveness and relatedness) strongly contributed to my saying to Ms. B. that I felt that there was a sadness in what we were talking about that had to do with the feeling that important aspects of her life were not being lived (were being "thrown away"). In referring to the sadness of a thrown away life, a life unlived, I was thinking not only of the way Ms. B. had not allowed herself to have the experience of being the mother of her (our) baby in the dream, but also of the way in which (to varying degrees) she had not allowed herself to live the experience of being in analysis with me and had not allowed herself to live the experience of being a daughter to her mother or of having a mother.

Ms. B. responded to what I said by crying in a way that felt to me that Ms. B. was experiencing sadness with me as opposed to dramatizing for me an invented feeling. She elaborated on the idea that much of her life had not been lived by telling me that she had to a large extent not experienced her life as a girl and as a woman since she had not had a sense of herself as having had a female body. As a result she felt she would never be able to "make milk for a baby." Implicit in this final statement of the hour was the patient's fear that she would never be able to fully experience being alive as a sexual woman with me and experience (in imagination) being mother of our baby.

Concluding Comment

There are of course innumerable lines of thought and feeling and levels of meaning in these three sessions that I have in my discussion either ignored altogether or only briefly and incompletely alluded to. Such is the nature of analytic work, especially analytic work in which one attempts to attend to the infinite complexity of the interplay of the unconscious life of the analysand and that of the analyst and to the ever-changing unconscious constructions generated in the "overlap" of the two. My intent has not been to be exhaustive in the explication of unconscious meanings, but to provide something of a sense of the rhythm of the to-and-fro of experiencing and reflecting, of listening and introspection, of reverie and interpretation, in analytic work that views the use of the analyst's reveries as a fundamental component of analytic technique.

7

On the Use of Language in Psychoanalysis

The subject of the use of language in psychoanalysis touches on virtually every aspect of psychoanalysis. In this chapter, I shall make no attempt to be encyclopaedic; rather, I shall offer a few tentative thoughts concerning the way in which the conscious and unconscious experience of analyst and analysand is conveyed/created (in large part through language) in the analytic setting. I shall discuss some implications for analysis of the idea that language is not simply a package in which communications are wrapped, but the medium in which experience is brought to life in the process of being spoken or written.

This chapter does not represent an effort to apply analytic thinking to the field of literary studies. Instead, I hope to make a small contribution to an awareness of the life of words (and the life in words) that occurs in the analytic situation. Rather than attempting to look behind language, the effort here is to look into it.

Reading, Writing, and Psychoanalysis

I shall begin in a way that I realize is more than a little odd for an analytic paper: I will attempt to describe something of my experience in the introductory English courses that I took when I was a student at Amherst College. My experience in those courses remains at the core of the way I approach the use of language both within and outside of the analytic setting.

The introductory writing course (required for all freshmen) was taught by the faculty of the English Department in sections of about fifteen students. The sections met three times per week for an academic year, and a paper of about a page-and-a-half in length (written in response to a given question) was to be submitted at each class meeting. The course began with the following writing assignment: "Describe a situation (real or imagined) in which you were being sincere." At each meeting of the class, a portion (at first, only a sentence) of several of the students' papers that had been written for the previous meeting were distributed, read aloud several times by the professor, and discussed. The effect of writing three of these papers each week was to generate the experience of continuous immersion in the process of writing for a full academic year. Writing and thinking about language became a way of life in a fashion not unlike the way in which the experience of being in analysis becomes "a way of life" for a period of time. The writing assignments continued:

- "Describe a situation in which you were being insincere."
- "In the situation you described in which you were insincere, how did you 'know' that you were being insincere?"
- "Describe a conversation in which you said something that felt insincere and then you changed a word or phrase or sentence, or even an intonation of voice which resulted in your feeling that what you had said was now more sincere. What was changed?"
- "What does the following statement mean to you: 'That was so unlike me like everything else I do.'"
- "Compose a letter in which you misrepresent something."
- "Compose a letter in which you try to correct a misunderstanding."
- "What is different about the writing in the two letters that you have written in the previous assignments?"

These were not exercises in psychology, semantics, rhetoric, linguistics, logic, or philosophy. They involved successive efforts at creating a setting in which each student could *listen to himself* in his efforts to use words and construct sentences in the process of attempting to express/create his thoughts and feelings in writing.

Although I had read some works by Shakespeare, Melville, Orwell, Hawthorne, Hemingway, and the like in high school, I had almost no sense of what was considered to be good, much less great, about their writing. (I'm not sure I ever really asked myself the question.) I remember with great clarity the first time I was able to hear in a student's paper the sound of good writing. In a paragraph being read aloud in the introductory writing class in the autumn of 1964, the student writer described feeling good one morning. As he walked down the sidewalk in front of his house, he said hello to a dog he passed. I cannot recall the precise words the student used in these sentences, but I heard and felt a vitality in the language that I had never heard before. With the age of the speaker unspecified in the paragraph, the writer had not only somehow conveyed in his language, a sense of what it is to feel light, but also had managed to capture an essence of what it feels like unselfconsciously to be a boy—a boy of five or a boy of sixteen, it didn't matter. I marveled at the way in which there was absolutely nothing imitative or posed about these sentences.

The place where style stopped and content began became increasingly difficult to determine with any certainty as the academic year progressed. The relationship between past and present also became interestingly complex: it began to seem that the past was in many ways only as real for oneself as the language one could create in the present. The inarticulateness of the past became palpable in its obstinate refusal to be reduced to words. The illusion of an "inner sincere self" that is tarnished by words seemed to break down. In its place began to emerge a sense that "sincerity" (a word whose meaning was continually slipping and sliding) was an experience inextricably linked with the way one uses language to make oneself known to oneself or to another person. I never articulated these ideas as such while in college (or for decades thereafter). It wasn't only that I couldn't have done so, I felt no inclination to try.

In retrospect, it seems that among the subjects being experimented with in this introduction to reading and writing was that of the interpenetration of one's experience, one's attempts to use language to communicate that experience, and the effect (on oneself and on other people) of the words one uses and the sentences one makes in that effort. The experiment in writing, reading, and listening that I have just described has a great deal in common with the experiment in thinking, feeling, and communicating that lies at the heart of the analytic experience. In the analytic hour, we rarely use writing as our medium of expression, but we do use words and we do use our developed capacities for listening to language (both to the patient's and to our own) in its spoken and unspoken forms.

"The Ear Does It"

In an effort to develop a vocabulary with which to think about and discuss the use of language in psychoanalysis, I would like to turn to an incident described by the literary critic Richard Poirier (1992) involving his fellow teacher and critic, Reuben Brower. The incident reflects something of an aesthetic sensibility that is common to Brower's approach to teaching students about reading poetry and to an approach to psychoanalysis to which I aspire:

> One year [Brower] began the course [an undergraduate course in the reading of English literature] with an exercise on a short poem by Edwin Muir, which, as an exasperated newcomer to the staff complained, simply "doesn't come together." This simply confirmed the wisdom of the choice for Brower, who said simply, "Well, let's see what they can do with it." "Do with it," not "Get out of it." The question he liked to ask on this and on other occasions was, again, simply "What is it like to read this poem?"—the very hardest of questions, and not one likely to encourage a search for coherent patterns. [p. 184]

The question "What is it like to read this poem?" focuses on *the experience of reading*, the experience of what it feels like to read, to listen to, to be spoken to (or written to) by the speaker/writer. I believe that there is an important and interesting overlap between the question "What is it like to read this poe.n?" and the question "What is it like to be with this patient?" For Brower (1951, 1968) the experience of reading is not most fundamentally a matter of uncovering "coherent patterns" of meaning hidden in the text which must be deciphered, decoded, or explicated; rather, the emphasis is on creating one's own words and sentences with which to describe the present moment created by the collision of author and reader. As important as is the process of understanding (in both the psychoanalytic experience and in the experience of reading), the process of not "know[ing] too much (Winnicott 1971, p.57) is at least as important. "Much better to practice the art of *not* arriving [at precise meaning]" (Poirier 1992, p. 182).

Once a poem, a novel, a play, an essay is written, the question of authorship and the (conscious) intention of the author recedes since the reader is author of his responses to what has been said or written. The poem, for example, having been written (the lines having been spoken) has done its work, and the reader/listener then becomes the creator of meanings, the author of his own sense of the poem as he experiences it (and has been changed by it), and (sometimes) attempts to find words with which to describe his experience of it. The reader/listener must somehow make the writing/speaking his own, or in Brower's terms, the reader must "see what he can do with it." In the process of writing, the poet must see what he can do with language in making something that captures, and in a sense creates in the moment of its "expression," something of what it feels like to be human "under certain circumstances" (H. James, *The Portrait of a Lady*, 1881, p.17).

The experience of writing and reading is not the same as the experience of being engaged in analysis. An effort to draw one-to-one correspondences between the two would constitute a type of reductionism that obscures the essence of each of these forms of human activity. Such a reduction of analysis to a type of "spoken literature" and analytic listening to a form of literary criticism is not at all what I have in mind when I attempt to make analytic use of the ideas of teachers of literature and literary critics. I am interested in the way such people think about and speak about encounters with other people's symbolic expressions/creations of the experience of being human.

Brower directs us to metaphor: "What is it *like* to read this poem?" (emphasis added). In posing this question, Brower asks us to bring to bear on the poem something new, something not already in the poem, but perhaps suggested by the poem's effect on us. In this way, the poem is actively engaged; we do something with it as opposed to understanding it.[1]

The analytic discourse requires of the analytic pair the development of metaphorical language adequate to the creation of sounds and meanings that reflect

---

1. I am reminded of Bion's comment to his analysand, James Grotstein, after Grotstein responded to one of Bion's interpretations by saying, "I understand." Bion paused and then calmly said, "Please try not to understand. If you must, superstand, circumstand, parastand, but please try not to understand" (Grotstein 1990, personal communication).

what it feels like to think, feel, and physically experience (in short to be alive as a human being to the extent that one is capable) at a given moment.[2] Such use of language is not an inborn capacity; it requires "ear training"[3] (Pritchard 1991) which the analyst provides from the very first meeting. The analyst, while attempting to avoid heavy-handed didacticism is, in important ways, very much like an English teacher in his efforts to enhance the patient's capacity for atunement to the subtlety of language as well as the enhancement of his capacity to use language in a way that more fully captures/creates his thoughts, feelings, perceptions, and so on in the analytic discourse.

In an initial meeting with an analysand, I said, "I am struck by the fact that you described our first

2. The analyst's creation of "metaphorical statements" constituting interpretations must not be an obtrusive event designed to demonstrate the analyst's cleverness with words. F. R. Leavis (1947), in his discussion of Milton, usefully distinguishes between a display of a "*feeling for words*" and the capacity to create "feeling *through* words" (p. 50).

3. Pritchard's term "ear training" is derived from language used by Robert Frost in a 1914 letter: "*The ear does it.* The ear is the only true writer and the only true reader. I have known people who could read without hearing the sounds and they were the fastest readers. Eye readers we call them. They can get the meaning by glances. But they are bad readers because they miss the best part of what a good writer puts into his words" (Frost 1914a, p. 677; quoted and discussed by Pritchard 1991, p.5).

phone conversation as if you weren't part of it." I
was speaking to her about the specifics of the way
in which her use of language had conveyed to me a
sense of what I imagined she had felt during our
phone call (and was speaking to her implicitly
about what I sensed she was currently feeling). The
analysand responded by asking me, "What do you
mean?" I said that it seemed that she must still feel
very anxious about whether it would be possible for
her to be part of an exchange with me. The patient
did not respond directly, but went on to speak in a
way that I gradually came to realize was imitative of
the way I speak, for example, in the halting
cadence of voice. I had the strange feeling of looking in a mirror and seeing myself while being
keenly aware of the insubstantial nature of the
reflection. I chose not to direct the patient's attention to her unconscious imitation of me because I
felt that to do so would have caused her to feel
painfully exposed. Instead, I listened to the
patient's "stories" (her presentation of her history).
In the course of this rather bland presentation of
herself, I found my mind wandering. I went over
my schedule for the day in my mind and struggled
to remember who I was to see in one of my afternoon hours. I eventually told the patient that I was
having difficulty getting a sense of what it felt like
to be her in the stories that she was telling me. The
patient said that she recognized her habit of "taking cover," but this acknowledgment had the effect

of sliding over what I suspected to be a far more troubling feeling—the feeling that what was being hidden was not her presence, but her absence. Toward the end of this hour and in succeeding hours, I began to broach with the patient the idea of her hidden absence and to link it with her question, "What do you mean?" I suggested that this question may have reflected an anxious (unconscious) effort to disguise from herself and from me a painful feeling of not being present.

I believe that analysis, although usually not overtly didactic, provides one of the most intense and rigorous experiences in "ear training" that human beings have created. (The analyst must perenially be aware of the danger that "teaching" of this type may slip into a form of indoctrination. To some degree the analysand's learning to speak the analyst's "tongue" [Balint 1968] in an inevitable feature of every analysis and must be addressed as an aspect of the transference-countertransference experience.)

In attempting to describe what I have in mind when I use the term "ear training," I shall briefly discuss the experience of listening to the use of language in a piece of writing, the opening sentence of Henry James' (1881) *The Portrait of a Lady*:

Under certain circumstances there are a few hours in life more agreeable than the hour dedicated to the ceremony known as afternoon tea. [p. 17]

This is an exquisite sentence (perhaps too exquisite), in which each word is chosen with all the care of
a master chef at an early morning market selecting
only those herbs and vegetables of the perfect size,
shape, color, texture, and fragrance. The words,
"Under certain circumstances" constitute a remarkable phrase with which to open a novel: this is precisely what a novel is concerned with—creating a voice
that will use language to describe what life is like
"under certain circumstances." But we are already
alerted to the fact that this is not just any voice or just
any life whose circumstances will be presented; it is a
life lived by someone who begins an account with this
elegant, knowing phrase that teeters on the edge of
pretentiousness. Perhaps it more than teeters—it may
already have begun its slide into self-satisfaction. The
effect is powerful and intriguing.

We read on: "Under certain circumstances, there
are few hours in life more agreeable . . ." The voice,
tone, and languid pace are sustained: ". . . there are few
hours in life more agreeable . . ." The words roll off the
tongue of a person who is fully at ease with language
and relishes the sounds that can be made with it:
indeed they are beautiful sounds. The word "agreeable" is perfect—it could not be "enjoyable," "pleasur-
able," or "relaxing"—the word "agreeable" is more
measured, more mature, more civilized.

The sentence (it is all one highly crafted sentence)
concludes: ". . . more agreeable than the hour dedicated to the ceremony known as afternoon tea." The
hour being described is not simply the hour when one

takes afternoon tea, it is "the hour dedicated to the ceremony known as afternoon tea." This "hour" (perhaps a play on the word "our") is no longer a measure of time; it is a measure of the development of Western civilization (which has been brought to its pinnacle in English culture). The hour is not simply "spent" or "passed" in a certain way, it is by this point in history "dedicated" not "to afternoon tea," but "to the ceremony known as afternoon tea." One does not ask the boorish question, "Known by whom?" It is known, and if one does not know, one need not read on. "We" are invited to smile with the speaker as we participate in the bond that joins us in our shared knowledge of the rich symbolism of the experience, an experience that has no equivalent.

There is at the same time a self-mockery and a gentle teasing of the reader as the speaker describes the "agreeable" ceremony with words chosen as artfully as one knows the speaker would make his selection from the tray of cakes we visualize before him. The voice is undeniably a voice of culture and taste, a voice so knowing, so civilized, so poised, that it is difficult to locate the person in it. The speaker is welcoming to the reader as a gracious host would welcome a guest who will share in the affectionate (very English) self-chiding we hear in the tone of this voice. But there is also an intelligence here so fierce that the reader can sense the challenge (even danger) of being pierced (from who knows where) by the gaze that is for the moment so seemingly cordial.

There is in the language constant movement, mystery, charm (in both the engaging and the manipulative sense of the word "charm") and a sense of the danger of being with such an unlocalizable intelligence (hardly even a person). This opening sentence does not feel like a satirical commentary on the last twig of the outermost branch of the evolutionary tree. Rather, it is a use of language in which human experience is not only being described, but is being created in the effect of the writing on the reader.

Reading and thinking about this opening sentence does not involve an effort to peer "behind" the language or "under" the words for hidden meanings; rather, it is an act of noticing the way in which language is being used. Meaning is *in* the language and the effects created by it. We listen *to* the language, not through it. As will be discussed later, this is precisely the direction an important strand of development of the theory of analytic technique is currently taking: there is a growing effort in contemporary analytic writing and practice to listen not only to what the patient is saying, but also to the way he is saying it and to the effect the patient is creating in the analytic relationship at any given moment (see, for example, Joseph 1975, 1982, 1985, Malcolm 1995, Ogden 1991a, Spillius 1995). Analysts are increasingly attempting to listen to the meanings generated, the effects created by the patient's use of language in addition to the semantic content of the language. There is currently far less emphasis on the attempt to look "behind" what the patient is saying for the story behind the story, the unconscious meaning "under" the conscious one. The unconscious is not "subconscious"; it is an aspect of the indivisible totality of consciousness. Similarly, meaning (including unconscious meaning) is *in* the language being used, not under it or behind it. (Freud [1915] believed the term "subconscious" to be "incorrect and misleading" [p. 170] since the Unconscious does not lie "under" consciousness.)

In the sentence from *The Portrait of a Lady* just discussed, we must allow ourselves not only to be "moved by the writing" (a largely passive description of the experience of reading), but must enter into an active *engagement with the writing* (and with the writer and the [imaginary] speaker). We must create the speaker (and ourselves in relation to him) as the writer gives us the "circumstances" in language with which to do this. Such is the nature of a form of human experience created through and in the medium of words. I am suggesting that this form of engagement with writing represents a quality of engagement (an aesthetic experience) that has much in common with the way in which we use ourselves as listeners, speakers, observers, and participants in the analytic encounter. Unless we can marvel at and enjoy the subtlety and complexity of the mind and the ways in which language is used in the analytic exchange, I think the practice of analysis could easily become a very dreary way to spend one's days.

A few brief comments on what it is that is unique to the analytic discourse (and what might be thought of as an "analytic aesthetic") may be useful in concluding this section. There are important areas of overlap and important differences between a literary aesthetic and an analytic aesthetic. I believe that what is essential to literature is the attempt to capture/create something *in* language that is significant about the experience of being alive as a human being and the enjoyment of the play of words and sentences through which this is made to happen. The capturing/creating of human experience in language is also of central importance to psychoanalysis. An analytic aesthetic, however, is also powerfully defined by the therapeutic function of psychoanalysis. The roles of analyst and analysand (and consequently the way each uses language to speak to the other) are structured by the purpose of their being together: the attempt to help the analysand effect lasting psychological change that will enable him to become more fully human.

The analysand's inability to lead a fuller (more human) life than he is currently capable of doing is often an outcome of his reliance on the (unconscious) methods by which he protects himself against real and imagined dangers. More specifically, the analytic task of helping the analysand become more fully human involves facilitating the patient's efforts (albeit ambivalent ones) to experience a greater range (and play) of thoughts, feelings, and sensations that are felt to be his own and that are felt to have been generated in the context of his own present and past relations with other human beings (including the analyst).

Given this conception of what it is that the analyst and analysand are about in their analytic work, the analytic discourse is not simply a discourse in which there is an attempt to capture/create in words something of the experience of being human; rather, it is, in addition, a discourse centrally concerned with creating language adequate to identifying and describing the *nature of the anxiety* at its "point of urgency" (Strachey 1934, p. 154) in the transference-countertransference that is preventing the analysand from experiencing a fuller range and greater play of thoughts, feelings, and sensations in the present moment. It is anxiety (psychic pain) that drives and directs the movement of the analytic dialogue. Analytic technique is guided by the effort to speak with the analysand about what it feels like for analyst and analysand to be with one another at that moment, it emphasizes the attempt to describe the most urgent fears that are shaping/constricting the analysand's capacity to experience that moment in a more fully human way.

The Analyst's Language

In addressing the analyst's use of language in the analytic dialogue, I bring to this topic a perspective that is somewhat at odds with the idea that the goal of the analyst in his use of language is to be as crisp, clear and clarifying as he can possibly be. Although I view this conception of the analyst's task as a partial truth, I feel that it must be held in tension with another partial truth: it is essential for the analyst to use language that aspires to a particular form of evocative, sometimes maddening, almost always disturbing, vagueness. In analysis, as in poetry, "Speech is not dirty silence/Clarified. It is silence made still dirtier" (Stevens 1947, p. 311). The analyst's language must embody in itself that there is no still point of meaning. Meaning is continuously in the process of becoming something new and in so doing, is continually undoing itself (undercutting its own claims to certainty). It is essential that the analyst's language embody the tension of forever being in the process of struggling to generate meaning while at every step casting doubt on the meanings "arrived at" or "clarified."

A patient about six months into analysis recently told me something that I take as high praise, although the patient did not consciously offer it as such: "You don't talk English. What you say is clear enough until I try to think about it. It's like no English I've ever heard. You choose your words very carefully, and in a way, they are unusually precise, but for some reason they are confusing. I almost always have the feeling that you've said more than what you seem to have said.

The analyst relies on language to upset (unsettle, decenter, disturb, perturb) the given—the given of the patient's conscious beliefs and narratives by which he creates illusions of permanence, certainty, and fixity of the experience of self and of the people who occupy his internal and external worlds. A central part of "the given" that is disturbed by language is the given of the patient's and the analyst's understanding of what is "going on" in the analytic relationship.

Language is at its most powerful when it disturbs, not by arriving at insights/understandings, but by creating possibilities: "billows or ripples of the stream of tendency" (Emerson 1841, p. 312). The analyst's language makes ripples in "the stream of tendency" in an effort to help analyst and analysand to break out of the circle of the eddy in which they are caught. The analytic pair never fully succeeds in this endeavor, but struggles in and through language to overcome itself (its own circling tendencies).

Lifelessness of analytic language

The variety of forms of lifelessness of analytic language is virtually endless. Among the most common that I have encountered is language that derives from dogmatism and ideological loyalties. When ideological bonds are dominant for the analyst, the analyst often adopts (or is adopted by) the language of his analytic "school." Analytic language that is ideological is no longer alive because the answers to the questions being raised are known by the analyst from the outset and the function of language has been reduced to the conveying of that knowledge to the analysand. Under such circumstances, there is a paucity of artfulness of language that "lives . . . upon experiment, upon uncer-

tainty, upon variety of attempt" (James 1884, pp. 44-
45). For example, the following two interpretations
made by analysts associated with different "schools" of
psychoanalysis were presented to me in the course of
consultation. In the face of a patient's consistently dismissing, paying lip service to, or ignoring virtually all
the analyst's interpretations, the analyst told the
patient, "You envy me my capacity to make linkages in
my mind, and you angrily attack each interpretation I
make because it reflects the fact that a dialogue, an
intercourse, has been going on in a place within me
over which you have no control and feel powerless."
Another analyst, in response to his patient's consistent
lateness to his sessions, observed, "You [the analysand]
have made no mention of the fact that you were again
late today to our meeting. You seem not to view this as
a way of defeating me and the analysis." Whether or
not such interpretations are accurate, well-timed,
addressed to the leading transference anxiety, and so
on, is academic. The language being used is so stale
that it ceases to address the experience that it purports
to address, that is, the patient's unconscious conflicts
and anxieties as externalized and experienced in the
transference-countertransference.

   The language of these interpretations is fundamentally a reflection of (and therefore a statement of)
a failure of imagination on the part of the analyst. The
analyst speaking in such ways has lost his capacity for
original thought and the ability to speak with his own
voice; he has given his mind and his use of language

over to someone else (real or imagined) and is often completely unaware that he has done so.

The analysts' language in these interpretations reflects the fact that they are speaking with a borrowed voice and are themselves mute. Such communications are indeed frightening ones that may lead the analysand to attempt to shield the analyst from awareness that the analyst has in a sense "lost his mind." The analysand may unconsciously endeavor to protect the analyst from awareness of this state of affairs by learning to speak the same cliché-ridden, stereotypic language. Under such circumstances, interpretations lose all vitality and instead sound like pre-packaged analytic theories being delivered by nobody in particular to nobody in particular.

One of my own failures of imagination was manifested by a period of consistently hackneyed thinking and formulaic use of language on my part. The analysand responded by telling me that the analysis had been going nowhere for several weeks, but that was not what worried him. He knew from his own experience in our work together and from his previous experiences in analysis that not every session or even every week of analysis was going to feel important or interesting. "What worries me, however, is my sense that you aren't worried by it." In this instance, the patient's interpretation not only was accurate, but it conveyed *in his use of language* all that had been absent. He was not only telling me, he was *showing me* with his words what it meant to use language in a lively way. The contempt

and condescension that oozed from his "generous for-
giveness" of the inevitable periods of stagnation in an
analysis both startled and embarrassed me.

This patient was ordinarily a man of few words,
and so the attention to detail in his wording of this relatively long statement was in itself a striking event that
punctuated the usual rhythm of our discourse. There
was dramatic tension in the structuring of his statement. He made me wait as his sentences gathered
momentum: this does not worry me, but what I am
about to point out *about you* does. Although such deri-
sive use of language can often seem strident, this
patient's comments did not feel shrill to me. In this
instance, I felt that the patient was attempting to talk to
me about something that was genuinely frightening to
him and secondarily maddening to him.

I felt embarrassed and humbled by his comments,
but most of all, awakened by them. The phrase "caught
with my pants down" went through my mind several
times. I was reminded of the fact that the analysand's
family had held regular "meetings" in which his parents
(as he had experienced it) had corrupted the very act of
talking by using words to "play mind games." The purpose of talk was to expose the patient's lack of intelligence (through his father's pointing out his misuse of
words) and to uncover the patient's unconscious motives
(for example, through his mother's "interpreting" his
wish to take the father's place as the head of the family).

I understood the patient's comment to me as, in
part, a reflection of the patient's identification with his

parents' sadistic use of "insight" and as a projective identification in which the sense of embarrassment, exposure, and emasculation were engendered in me. As important, the patient's interpretation seemed to me to be an attempt to bring the analysis to life again by alerting me to (creating in me) a sense of the way in which talking could be corrupted and could become not only useless, but destructive. In this instance, my own interpretations did not at first seem to me to be sadistic. Instead, they seemed to have been an imitation of analysis in that they reflected the fact that I was not emotionally present, but was pretending to be so in my use of formulaic language. Later in the analysis, I came to appreciate the way in which my withdrawal into "playing at analysis" (as reflected in my formulaic use of language) also represented an unconscious identification with a sadistic/self-protective way in which the patient had tormented his parents in childhood and continued to torment (and shield himself from) his unconscious internal object parents. By imitating a connection with them, he could (in unconscious fantasy) become invisible and unreachable and could induce in them impotent rage. In the analysis, I had unwittingly participated in an unconscious intersubjective construction (the "analytic third" [Ogden 1994a, b]) in which I had come to experience myself and behave (for example, in my use of formulaic language) in a way that was congruent with the unreachable/tormenting/ self-protective aspect of the patient's internal object relationship.

Dead language (for example, stereotypic, cliché-ridden, over-inflated, authoritarian language) regularly reflects the fact that the analyst at that moment has nothing to say to the analysand in his own voice, from his own mind, in his own words. Whether the source of the problem is dogmatic attachment to an analytic school of thought or a reflection of unwitting participation in a transference-countertransference drama as in the clinical example just presented, the analyst often has very little mind of his own with which to generate a thought or to create language in which a multiplicity of possible meanings exists. Creating language with one's own voice is itself an act of freedom that is a necessary condition for the creation of an analytic setting in which psychological change may occur: "This struggle for verbal consciousness should not be left out in art. It is a very great part of life. It is not superimposition of a theory. It is the passionate struggle into conscious being" (Lawrence 1919, p. x). I am suggesting that the analyst must actively struggle with language in an effort to create ideas and sentences and a voice of his own with which to speak them. This struggle to convey one's experience with one's own words, in one's own voice is a very large part of what it means to be alive in an analytic relationship.

Creating Effects in Language

In the final section of this chapter, I will focus on some of the ways in which effects created in the use of language serve as a central medium of communication of unconscious experience in the analytic setting. Effects created *in language* of course coexist with the use of language to name, describe, and in other ways speak about one's experience. When I refer to effects created in language, I am placing emphasis on a dimension of language usage in which the creation and communication of meanings/feelings is indirect, that is, relatively independent of what is being said (at the level of the semantic content of language). Such effects in language are always in movement, always in the process of occurring, "always on the wing, so to speak and not to be glimpsed except in flight" (Wm. James 1890, p. 253).

Few have described as eloquently as William James (1890) in *Principles of Psychology*, the way in which language fails to convey meaning (especially affective meaning) when it is used in a fashion that is focused on what it is saying as opposed to what it is doing. James discusses what he felt to be a pull in our use of language toward the "substantives" of language (the nouns around which the meanings of sentences tend to be organized). Feelings, especially those without names ("all *dumb* or anonymous psychic states") tend to get lost "in thoughts 'about' this object or 'about' that, the stolid word *about* engulfing all their delicate idiosyncrasies in its monotonous sound" (James 1890, p. 246). James believed that human experience is captured/expressed in language not so much through the power of its "substantives" to name or describe (to speak "about"), but more indirectly, through the elements of language (more accurately, *in* language) that contribute to the creation of a sense of movement and transition, "a feeling of relation moving to its term" (p. 244). It is the "transitive parts" (p. 243) of language, "the places of flight" (p. 243), that come closest to capturing something of the texture and the aliveness of felt feelings and the movement of "the stream of thought" (p. 243):

> There is not a conjunction or a preposition, and hardly an adverbial phrase, syntactic form, or inflection of voice in human speech, that does not express some shading or other which we at some moment actually feel to exist between the larger objects [the substantives] of our thought . . . [p. 246]

Struggling to break out of the confines of content-centered use of language, James suggests,

> We ought to say a feeling of *and*, a feeling of *if*, a feeling of *but*, and a feeling of *by*, quite as readily as we say . . . a feeling of *cold*. Yet we do not: so inveterate has our habit become of recognizing the existence of the substantive parts alone, that language almost refuses to lend itself to any other use. [pp. 245-246]

Thus, James attempts to explore the ways in which language can be used *to do* what it cannot say. Similarly, it is through effects created in language in an analytic setting that meanings/feelings are created and conveyed that lie beyond what is being said. It is precisely this aspect of analytic communication that is at the heart of the current elaboration and extension by Joseph (1975, 1982, 1985) and others of Klein's (1952) concept of transference as "total situation." It is increasingly widely recognized that in order to "catch the drift" (Freud 1923a) of the unconscious internal object world of the analysand, we must "think in terms of *total situations* transferred from the past to the present" in addition to the transferring of specific "emotional defenses and object relations" (Klein 1952, p. 55). In this way, Klein began to shift the focus of our theoretical and technical treatment of transference from the content of what is being transferred (the Jamesian "substantives") to the *totality of the effect* of transference experience in/on the analytic relationship. To a large extent, these effects are created in the patient's use of language "alongside and beyond what he is saying" (Joseph 1985, p. 447).[4]

In the following brief clinical discussion, I shall attempt to provide a sense of the way in which effects in language are generated in an analytic setting.

The analysand, an academic in her late 30's, had been "terminated" from two previous analyses when (in both instances) the analyst became

---

4. I believe that transference as total situation is perhaps more accurately conceived of as "transference-countertransference as total situation."

enraged with her and informed her that she was
unanalyzable. Although the patient was highly
respected by her colleagues for the quality of her
work, she derived little pleasure from it. Music and
painting were the passions of her life and occupied
almost all of her time outside of work.

The patient filled session after session with
stories about events in her life and did not seem to
mind that I said very little. Interpretations that I
did offer were politely tolerated. The analysand
seemed relieved, however, when I had finished saying what I had to say so that she could return to
"filling me in" on what she had been talking about.
She would repeat almost verbatim stories that she
had told me on many previous occasions. In a session occurring about six months into the analysis, I
said to the patient that it seemed to me that she
must feel that I was not listening to her and that I
remembered very little of what she told me. The
patient, as usual, ignored what I said and returned
to the account that I had "interrupted."

It took me almost a year to understand something of the way in which the patient was unconsciously using language, not for the purpose of
talking to me about what she was thinking, feeling,
perceiving, experiencing in her body, and so on,
but to create an effect *in language*: the experience
of wrapping herself in the pure sensation sound of
words. At the same time, the effect created in me
by this use of language (the countertransference

aspect of the unconscious transference-counter-transference construction) was the experience of being utterly useless and without currency for the patient. As I came to understand this dimension of the transference-countertransference (by treating the effects created in language as vehicles for understanding the patient's unconscious experience), I was able to restrict myself to serving as a (potentially) human medium in whose (almost entirely unfelt) presence the patient could engage in relatedness to an "autistic shape" (the sensation of the sound of her own words) (Tustin 1984; see also Ogden 1989a, b). All of the patient's previous experience of relatedness to autistic shapes (for example, painting and listening to music) had been done in isolation.

Some three years into the analysis, there were fleeting indications that the patient had begun to develop a dim awareness of my presence. For example, during this period, she "complimented" me in a double edged way for my remarkable listening abilities. I experienced this comment as the patient's indirectly telling me that she felt that I had said very little to this point that had been of any value to her. It seemed to me that the analysand was unconsciously asking me to challenge more vigorously her self-imposed isolation in her sensation-dominated world (even though she felt grateful to me for thus far not having interfered with her self-soothing activities). Over time I was able to describe for her my experience of her using words *not to talk to me* and in fact not to be alive with me. I added that her wrapping herself in the sensation of the sound of her own voice seemed to help her to reduce herself to a series of pure physical sensations. She seemed in the course of her life to have developed the capacity to turn herself into a structure so dense that practically all movement, all life, seemed to be extinguished.

In this patient's analysis, it was critical that I be able to learn that transference-countertransference meaning lay most importantly in the effects created by the patient's use of words not to communicate, not to think, not to create/convey feeling, but to generate a necessary, but virtually lifeless, insulating sensory medium.

Concluding Comments

A central task of psychoanalysis today involves continuing to develop a use of language that is adequate to the task of capturing/creating the experience of "what it feels like" for the analyst to be with the patient and for the patient to be with the analyst at a particular juncture. It has been my experience that the language of both patient and analyst is dead (and thinking and communicating cease) when their use of language conveys certainty as opposed to tendency, knowledge as opposed to a tentative, ever-sliding sense of things, fixity as opposed to movement and transition.

A significant strand of the recent history of psycho-
analysis is the story of the development of the analyst's
appreciation of the importance of the way in which
effects created in language (what the patient's language
does "alongside and beyond" what it says) represent an
important medium in which the communication of
unconscious experience occurs.

8

Listening: Three Frost Poems

Joseph Brodsky (1995a) has referred to poetry as "a great disciplinarian" (p. 100) to prose. I would add that poetry is a great disciplinarian to analytic listening. In this chapter I will look at the way language is used in the making of poetry in three Frost poems. My interest is not so much in what a poem is "about," but rather in what a poem is. I will be discussing the ways effects are created in language and how these effects taken together create the unique experience the reader generates (with the poet) in listening to the poem.

I have written this chapter for the sheer pleasure of reading and writing about poetry and I offer it to the reader in that spirit. It is a chapter that has been written without concern that it be "useful" to the analytic reader. (I will leave it entirely to the reader to make what connection, if any, he or she is inclined to make between the experience of listening to poetry and the experience of listening to the language created in an analytic relationship.) Perhaps if this chapter does not aspire to being "useful," the reader and I might be sufficiently free to make anything and nothing of it. The poet A.R. Ammons (1968) has put it far better than I am able to in his comparison of poetry to a walk:

> You could ask what walks are good for. . . . Walks are useless. So are poems. . . . A walk doesn't mean anything, which is a way of saying that to some extent it means anything you can make it mean— and always more than you can make it mean. . . . Only uselessness is empty enough for the presence of so many uses. . . . Only uselessness can allow the walk to be totally itself. [pp. 118–119]

I will not attempt to get "behind" the language being discussed, but will attempt to get into the language as deeply as I am able and to allow it to get deeply into me. I will experiment with a variety of ways of thinking and speaking about three Frost poems. Of particular interest to me are the effects created by the sound and meanings of these words and sentences and the way language is used to create these effects. Put another way, I will be discussing what it is "like to read this poem" (Brower, quoted by Poirier 1992, p. 184) and how the poem enlists me and how I enlist the poem as I "say the lines" (Frost 1962, p. 911).

Before turning to the poems themselves, I would like to briefly comment on two interrelated topics: the changes in the way Frost's poetry has been viewed since his death in 1963 and the difficulty posed by the speaking voice in Frost's poetry. Although Frost achieved wide recognition as a poet, including being awarded four Pulitzer prizes, there was a general feeling among literary critics that he was a "people's poet," a cultural figure comparable to Carl Sandberg or Edgar Lee Masters. His popularity, it was felt, was due to his folksiness and to catchy lines (for example, "Good fences make good neighbors") that made his poetry easily grasped by the general public. The quality of Frost's poetry did indeed decline as his popularity grew (Jarrell 1953, Poirier 1977). He seemed in the last two decades of his life to have developed a formula that he used repeatedly to the detriment of his poetry. This contributed to his relegation by literary critics to the ranks of the "less than great" poets.

It has been only gradually over the past forty or fifty years that Frost has increasingly come to be viewed differently by critics, academics, and poets (including Auden, Brodsky, Heaney, Jarrell, Lowell, and Wilbur). Randall Jarrell (1953) was among the first poets and literary critics to identify and write compellingly about "the other Frost" (p. 26). In one of his pithy (and more than a little condescending) one-liners, Jarrell remarked, "Ordinary readers think Frost is the greatest poet alive, and love some of his best poems almost as much as they love some of his worst ones" (p. 26). Jarrell's reference to "ordinary reader" was directed as much to "ordinary" literary critics and academics as to the "ordinary" members of the general public. Almost beseechingly, Jarrell asks the reader to actually read the poems before dismissing them: "Nothing I say about these poems can make you see what they are like, or what the Frost that matters most is like; if you read them you will see" (p. 27). Jarrell concludes his two remarkable essays on Frost by saying,

> To have the distance from the most awful and the most nearly unbearable parts of the poems, to the most tender, subtle, and loving parts, a distance so great; to have this whole range of being treated with so much humor and sadness and composure . . . to see that a man can still include, connect, and make humanly understandable or humanly ununderstandable so *much*—this is one of the freshest and oldest of joys. . . . [p. 62]

But the impact of the "discovery" of the "other Frost" by Jarrell (who was himself peripheral to academia), was not nearly as significant an event in literary circles as Lionel Trilling's description of Frost in 1959 as "a terrifying poet" (quoted by Brodsky 1995b, pp. 224–225). Poirier's (1977) critical study of Frost's poetry and Pritchard's (1984) reconsideration of Frost's literary life were pivotal to the shift that has occurred in the way Frost's poetry is read and the esteem in which he is held as a poet.

My own response to Frost's poetry has roughly paralleled the movement just described (although occurring much later). I read a good deal of Frost in college and during the years afterwards, but was not taken by what I read. The speaking voice in the poems (as I look back on it) seemed to present a narrative that was so clear that it seemed to leave me little to do as a reader. I was more drawn to "difficult" modern poets such as Eliot, Pound, Stevens, Marianne Moore, and William Carlos Williams. Frost is not a "difficult" poet in Eliot's sense of the word[1]; his poetry does not dislocate by means of disjointed or absent narrative, fragmented images, obscure literary allusions, and so on. However, Frost's poetry is indeed difficult, but difficult in ways quite different from Eliot, Pound, and the others. His poems are difficult in large part because they "suggest formulae that won't formulate—that almost but don't quite formulate. I should like to be so subtle . . . as to seem to the casual reader altogether obvious" (Frost 1917).

In Frost's (1942b) poem, "The Most of It" (which in an earlier draft was titled "Making the Most of It"), a

---

1.   Eliot's views on poetry held enormous sway in literary circles and in academia during the period of Frost's maturity as a poet and for a decade or so afterwards. The following passage from Eliot's (1921) essay, "The Metaphysical Poets," had a great deal to do with what was in fashion for many decades: ". . . it appears likely that poets in our civilization, as it exists at present, must be *difficult*. . . . The poet must become more and more comprehensive, more allusive, more indirect, in order to force, to dislocate if necessary, language into his meaning" (p. 248).

man calls across a lake and bemoans the fact that
nature merely offers up a "mocking echo" and refuses
to respond with a "counter-love" of its own. The man
continues to look across the lake,

> As a great buck it powerfully appeared,
> Pushing the crumpled water up ahead,
> And landed pouring like a waterfall,
> And stumbled through the rocks with horny tread,
> And forced the underbrush—and that was all.
> [p. 307]

A large part of the "difficulty" encountered in reading Frost is reflected in the final four words of this
poem, "and that was all." Frost's poetry lives in the
realm of "and that was all," and resists as if willfully our
efforts to make it (the poem, the world, our lives) mean
something more than "that." But what is "that"? At first
"and that was all" seems like the poet's wise, unsenti-
mental, pragmatic insight into man's relationship with
nature: an echo is an echo, a buck is a buck, no more
and no less. But on closer inspection, what appeared to
be wisdom, feels more and more like a rather common-
place, self-evident statement (a horse is a horse) that
mocks us as the echo was felt to mock the man in the
poem. What is interesting about the ending of the
poem is the unexpected appearance at the very end of
this twenty-line poem of a new voice appearing out of
the silence (following the dash) much as the buck unexpectedly emerged from the lake. The reader, like the

man in the poem, cannot resist wishing the poem would "speak to him" and consequently attempts to make the words "and that was all" a memorable, simple truth that he can wrap up and take home with him. But the buck in the poem is more than a buck and less; it is a buck that is the creation of the poem. It is a buck that pushes "the crumpled water up ahead" and lands "pouring like a waterfall." It is not a buck "out there" in nature, but a buck created in the poem through the sounds of "newly made" words and imaginative metaphor.

The voice in the final phrase of the poem is ironic, witty, and rather detached and, like the buck, appears for only a moment before disappearing into the underbrush. It is a voice that will not be pinned down; it is only fleetingly glimpsed, and never to be owned (known). It is the elusiveness and subtlety of this voice that is a large part of what makes Frost's poetry so difficult, so interesting, so alive and present and yet always somehow just out of reach.

I will now turn to three Frost poems, "The Silken Tent," "Home Burial" and "I Could Give All to Time." I have chosen these poems because I am very fond of them, each for different reasons, but none in its entirety. Each has its moments of aliveness and moments of flatness; the parts that are most alive for me change over time. (It is important that the reader read these poems aloud several times before going on to my discussion for the poems live in the sounds of the words and in what the words feel like in our mouths as we say them.)

I.

The "Silken Tent" (1942c) was first published in a volume of Frost's poems titled, *A Witness Tree*. The title of the volume is taken from the name given to a tree that marks (stands witness to) a property line and is "My proof of being not unbounded" (Frost, 1942d, p. 301).

The Silken Tent

She is as in a field a silken tent
At midday when a summer breeze
Has dried the dew and all its ropes relent,
So that in guys it gently sways at ease,
And its supporting central cedar pole,
That is its pinnacle to heavenward
And signifies the sureness of the soul,
Seems to owe naught to any single cord,
But strictly held by none, is loosely bound
By countless silken ties of love and thought
To everything on earth the compass round,
And only by one's going slightly taut
In the capriciousness of summer air
Is of the slightest bondage made aware.

Frost (1923) spoke of poetry as "words that have become deeds" (p. 701). "The Silken Tent" often succeeds in becoming a "deed" in the sense of becoming an experience itself as opposed to a description of a feeling or of an experience. In the opening line, "She is as in a field a silken tent," what is being compared to the silken tent is not "She," but "She is" (an active quality of being, more verb than pronoun). How different the poem would have been had Frost begun the poem with the words, "She is like," instead of "She is as." The word "as" is itself a lighter, less angular word than "like" and invites a much softer comparison. After the opening word, "She" is never again mentioned and instead remains as if suspended over the line and then over the entirety of the poem.

The graceful unity and integrity of the tent is captured far less in the description of the tent than in the reader's sensory experience of the poem being woven from the slender thread of a single uninterrupted sentence. The poem never rests: there is continual movement generated in the play of hardness and softness, of expansiveness and boundedness. In the opening four lines, we feel the way the soft "s" sounds of the words (for example, "So that in guys it gently sways at ease") are gently, but firmly, held in place by the taut structure of the meter, rhythm and rhyming pattern of the sonnet form. Even in the space of two words in line three "ropes relent" the reader can experience the hardness and density of the word "ropes" giving way a bit, but just a bit, to the looser feel of the broader two-syllabled word "relent" with its soft "l" and slightly rounded "t" sounds.

There is a shift in the sound and rhythm of the words (and with it a slight shift in mood) as the poem moves from the opening four lines to the three that follow. The fifth line ("And its supporting central cedar pole") requires that we stop after each word in a way that seems to "line up" the words and sounds. It is not possible to say the words, "And its supporting central cedar pole," without pausing after the words "supporting," "central," and "cedar." (At the same time, the alliteration of these three words gently ties them together.) A sense of "verticality" is created that stands in contrast to the smooth "horizontal" swaying movement of the previous line.

The poem in lines six and seven takes on an almost reverential tone. The cedar pole is implicitly compared to a church spire (a pinnacle) reaching upward. The poem seems to swell here (in a way that I find a bit humorless) as it reaches beyond the personal to the universal. But even as the poem takes on this quasi-religious expansiveness, the image of the central cedar pole inside of and protruding through the silken fabric has a delicate, but unmistakably sexual quality.

By the middle of the poem, the silken tent has taken on a life of its own and we hardly remember that the tent is "just a simile" for who "She is." In the phrase, "silken ties of love and thought," the poem playfully comes around on itself as human feelings and capacities are used as metaphors for the movement and structure of an object (the tent) which in turn is a simile for the essence of a human being. In this way, the tent imagery is "drawn back in" as if by cords that loosely bind. The effect created by the clause "loosely bound/ By countless silken ties of love and thought" is for me the most interesting and vital moment in the poem. The word "thought" is unexpected and rescues the line and the next one from feeling like standard poetical form. The word "thought" re-humanizes the tent simile even more than the more "poetical" word "love." There is a fullness to the word "thought" in that it evokes a sense of thoughtful considerateness as well as a quality of liveliness of mind. The liveliness of mind is not simply named, but is a felt presence in the liveliness of the play of words, in the vitality of images and metaphors gracefully and sensuously bending and circling within one another, in the immense pleasure taken in performing, witnessing, and experiencing a feat of language flawlessly carried off.

The poem concludes,

> And only by one's going slightly taut
> In the capriciousness of summer air
> Is of the slightest bondage made aware.

The tie to who "She is" is maintained here by the ambiguity of the word "one's" which refers to both one cord and to the feeling of one person. We can experience in our bodies the lightness of air as we feel our breath carrying the final syllable of the poem, that is itself air ("-are") tenderly held inside the softness of the word "aware."

"The Silken Tent" is an exquisitely beautiful love poem. But it is an odd love poem in that "She," the beloved, is so quickly and thoroughly displaced by the

silken tent that we at times forget her, and yet it doesn't
seem to matter that we have forgotten her. I think that
this is so because in an important sense "She" is the
poem, or perhaps more accurately, "She is" (her being is)
the experience of making poetry. When I have asked
myself what it might feel like to receive this love poem, my
immediate response has regularly been that I would
much prefer to be its writer than its recipient. For me, the
poem better succeeds in capturing an essence ("the
soul") of the love of poetry than it succeeds in capturing
the experience of the love of a person or of the love of a
perception of beauty in nature. The delicate tensions that
are both the subject of and the life of this poem are the
tensions at the heart of poetry itself—the forever unresolved "pulls" between passion and restraint, between
expansiveness and boundedness, the revealed and the
hidden, simplicity and complexity, surface and depth, the
spoken, the unsaid, and the merely suggested.

This poem, that makes words and the experience
of the love of poetry as light as air, is always doing more
than that. From the outset, the language and imagery
softly, but insistently suggest an awareness of the tem-
porality of the experience being created in the poem.
The tent is a silken tent, a delicate fabric, "at midday,"
subject to "the capriciousness of summer air" (perhaps
a metaphor for the capriciousness of human emotion).
An experience (of a person, of a perception of beauty,
of a poem) cannot be made to stand still and will never
again be what it is in this moment. A poet (or a reader
of poetry) cannot know if he will ever again be able to

make a good poem or allow a poem to get deeply into him. This awareness is an inextricable part of the language of the poem and of the fabric of the experience of love. In the final words of the final line, the word "bondage" seems to insist on being heard as a darker, heavier word than those used earlier to refer to the element of restraint: "guys," "held," "bound," "ties," "taut." The word "bondage," even as it is being used in a phrase creating a sense of delicate lightness, has an ominous sound that is a reminder that passion is as enslaving as it is freeing. As Frost well knew, the poet's passion for making poems is his prison (in a very unromantic sense) as well as his vital core.

II.

Frost's (1914b) "Home Burial" may be one of the most successful efforts in American poetry to capture in verse the sound and feeling of people talking to one another. A transcript of an actual dialogue captures only what was said and as a result conveys only a small part of what it feels like being there listening and watching. A major part of the poet's attempt to write dialogue in poetry involves the effort to capture in the action of the language itself the living sound and experience of speech. Frost (1913) believed that the vitality of speech is in its sound, "the sound of sense": "The best place to get the abstract [pure] sound of sense is from voices behind a door that cuts off the words" (p. 80). In order to achieve this, the sentences must "talk

to each other as two or more people do in a drama"
(Frost 1936, p. 427) so that the poem is not simply a
representation of a dialogue but is itself a dialogue.

"Home Burial" is one of Frost's longer poems and
so I will focus only on the way the poem begins. This is
a poem in which a couple wrestles with the death of
their first child who is buried in a small family gravesite
at the side of their home.

Home Burial

He saw her from the bottom of the stairs
Before she saw him. She was starting down,
Looking back over her shoulder at some fear.
She took a doubtful step and then undid it
To raise herself and look again. He spoke
Advancing toward her: 'What is it you see
From up there always—for I want to know.'
She turned and sank upon her skirts at that,
And her face changed from terrified to dull.
He said to gain time: 'What is it you see,'
Mounting until she cowered under him.
'I will find out now—you must tell me, dear.'
She, in her place, refused him any help
With the least stiffening of her neck and silence.
She let him look, sure that he wouldn't see,
Blind creature; and awhile he didn't see.
But at last he murmured, 'Oh,' and again, 'Oh.'

'What is it—what?' she said.

                                    'Just that I see.'

The poem opens plainly and yet convulsively as an essence of a complex relationship between two people is in an instant created in the sounds and movement of the words:

He saw her from the bottom of the stairs
Before she saw him. She was starting down,
Looking back over her shoulder at some fear.

The first line is confusing and deeply disturbing to me each time I read the poem. In reading the words "He saw her from the bottom of the stairs/Before she saw him," my disorientation is so great that as often as not, I stop and begin again in an attempt to get the language and image to stand still. There are three people in the scene I tell myself: a man, a woman, and the speaker. But I cannot see them in my mind. Who is where? Seeing is everything ("He saw her . . . she saw him") and yet the reader struggles unsuccessfully to see, as if peering through dim light.

The phrase "She was starting down" has in the sequence and pitch of the sound of the words a movement forward and downward from "She" with its long "e" sound to the resonant lower tones of the word "down." But the following line, "Looking back over her shoulder at some fear," superimposes movement in the opposite direction thus creating a contorted image of movement forward and backward, downward and upward, into the future and into the past. The words "some fear" stand out in these opening three lines. The

word "fear" is unexpected (" 'fetched' . . . from its regular place" [Frost 1918, p. 696] since we rarely think of
ourselves as turning to look at an abstraction such as a
fear or a hope or a joy. The effect is greatly enhanced
by the use of the word "some" as a modifier since this
word, instead of telling us more about the fear, seems
to obstruct our view by refusing to name it or even
describe it.

The poem continues,

> She took a doubtful step and then undid it
> To raise herself and look again.

In the first of these lines, the regularity of the
cadence of iambic pentameter[2] is subtly altered. A
"doubtful step" is created in the sound of the language
by adding an extra unstressed syllable to the end of the
line. In this way, a sense of stumbling, of "falling off the
end of the line," is heard and felt in one's voice as one
says the line.[3] In addition, there is dark irony in the line
"She took a doubtful step and then undid it." Unstated,

---

2.   Iambic pentameter is a poetic cadence consisting of five "feet"
(metrical units) per line with each foot consisting of an unstressed
syllable followed by a stressed syllable. Frost (1939) often
remarked that in English (unlike in French, Russian, or any other
language) "there are virtually but two [meters], strict iambic and
loose iambic" (p. 776).

3.   I am indebted to Alice Jones, a poet who has taught me something about meter and a great deal about a passion for poetry.

but implicit here is the knowledge (starkly framing the entire poem) that while steps might be retraced and actions reconsidered, nothing is ever undone.

> He spoke
> Advancing toward her: 'What is it you see,
> From up there always—for I want to know.'

The reader, too, is advancing toward her: our "hearing" the husband's spoken words, "What is it you see" in his own voice and in his own words creates the effect of a cinematic movement from a more distant viewing angle to a close-up shot. We can hear and feel in our mouths in saying the word "always" the elongation of the speaking voice that stands in contrast to the nervous staccato effect of the eight monosyllabic words that precede it. The word "always" captures a sense of the timelessness (not simply repetitiveness) of what is occurring. Consider the difference it would make if the line read, "What is it you always see from up there?" The placement of the word "always" at the end of the phrase, just before the long pause created by the dash allows the sound of the word "always" to reverberate and then to die in the caesura that follows the word. It is as if the sound of the word "always" is made to echo in the stony silence of the vast emptiness of a house that this couple is no longer able to fill.

The use of the word "always" is as unexpected to the reader as were the words "some fear." But here there is, in addition, a sense that the husband too did not expect to hear himself utter that word. He pauses after saying it as if attempting to absorb the immense sadness that he hears in the sound of the word that came from his mouth. The silence after the word "always" transforms the words that follow: "For I want to know." The reader (and, we imagine, the husband too) had anticipated hearing an anxious, impatient demand in these words. The words following the break in the line seem to have been uttered rather reflexively as if left over from a state of mind that no longer exists. The husband, having heard the sound of the word "always" echoing in the emptiness of the silence (the empty house) is now, despite himself, making a much more complex expression of feeling with these reflexive words than anything he (or the reader) could have expected. The words "For I want to know" now seem to reflect the way in which the husband has begun to sense, despite his persistent questioning, that he does not want to know, and yet in some way already does "know." (The word "know," in a highly compacted way, captures in its sound the fearful objection, "No," that in this poem lives in the very bowels of the wish to know.)

> She turned and sank upon her skirts at that,
> And her face changed from terrified to dull.

The wife's silence and body movements are powerfully expressive of her withdrawal into abject despair. There is a flattening, a dulling of the language here. It is descriptive in that it is telling us "about" what is happening as opposed to the more immediate, more lively experience of hearing what is occurring in the sound of the husband's voice.

> He said to gain time: 'What is it you see,'
> Mounting until she cowered under him.

The most interesting and telling words in these lines are in the conjunctive phrase "to gain time." This phrase creates a feeling of a person being in two places at once: the husband is ahead of and behind himself in that he already in some inarticulate way "knows" the answer to the question he is about to ask again, but needs time to attempt to "know" in a different way, that is, in a way that names and is engaged in the work of wrestling with what he already knows. Ironically, time is something that he cannot "gain" in the world of "always" in which he and his wife and their child are trapped.

The words "mounting" and "cowering" in the second of these two lines suggest a subverted intercourse in which two people resist experiencing "something human" (to use a phrase from the middle of the poem) in one another. The title of the poem, "Home Burial" is accruing meanings as the poem unfolds, including by this point, a sense not only of a burial at home, but also a burial of a home, of a family, of a marriage. It is a "terrifying" burial in that the husband and wife have (in a sense that we are experiencing in the language) been buried alive. (There is grim humor in the play on

words in the title that reflects the disturbing detachment of the even handed, never-taking-sides quality of
the narrative voice in this poem.)

The husband repeats his question, which is no
longer a question, but a demand that his wife name
what he already "knows," but cannot bear to make
more real for himself by naming it:

'I will find out now—you must tell me, dear.'

The word "dear" rings so hollow that it is chilling.
In the entire blank verse poem of more than a hun-
dred-and-twenty lines there is only one instance of hard
rhyming of line-ending words (other than a word rhyming with itself). The single instance occurs in the rhyming of the word "dear" in this line with the word "fear"
almost a dozen lines earlier. In this way, the poem subtly does in language what the couple is doing to one
another: it infects (links) the love that they at one time
felt ("dear") with the fear that is consuming them both.

She, in her place, refused him any help
With the least stiffening of her neck and silence.

The phrase "in her place" is a curious one in that
in three monosyllabic words it succeeds in creating a
sense of the way the husband and wife have each taken
(or rather, have been taken by) an immobile "place"
that is ruled by a feeling of "always." I am regularly
caught off guard by the word "least" in the phrase "the

least stiffening of her neck." The word (like almost everything else that is going on in this poem) seems to be pulling against itself. There is a refusal on the part of the wife to help her husband (or herself) that is conveyed by even the least stiffening of her neck (her refusal is contained in every sinew of her body); and at the same time, there is a modulation of the refusal in that it is *only* a slight stiffening of her neck.

> She let him look, sure that he wouldn't see,
> Blind creature; and awhile he didn't see.

The words "Blind creature" attain added power as the voice of the wife burns through into the detached narrative voice. The semicolon after the hate-filled words "Blind creature" creates another silence during which we wait both with the wife in her impatient, foot-tapping anger and with the husband in his tortured struggle with himself. (Silence, the space between the words, is in this poem at least as expressive as the words themselves.)

The vague impenetrability of the words "some fear" are also accruing meaning and in these lines have come to suggest that the wife, in looking over her shoulder, is not experiencing the death of her child so much as she is seeing her fear of experiencing that loss. Despite the fact that her gaze is fixed "always" on the grave, she, like her husband, cannot see it (in the sense of being able to experience it, to allow it its full realness and finality, and to grieve over it). There is a subtle

ambiguity to the epithet "Blind creature" in that it
refers not only to the husband's (perceived) inhuman-
ity reflected in his inability to "see," but also to the
wife's inhumane blindness to her husband's (and her
own) tortured attempts to mourn.

> But at last he murmured, 'Oh,' and again, 'Oh.'
> 'What is it—what?' she said.
>   'Just that I see.'

The rhythm of the first of these lines is remarkable
in the way that the words (with the help of the pauses
and silences generated by three commas and a period
in the space of four words) move at a painfully slow
pace as the husband "at last" murmurs, " 'Oh,' and
again, 'Oh.'" The sounds are those of an involuntary
moan of pain. The word "creature" in the previous line
now takes on a surprising softness almost despite itself
as the sound we hear is like that of a trapped, wounded
animal (creature). The pace quickens in the second of
these lines as the words carry the bitter, prickly, hard-
ened voice of the wife (" 'What is it—what?' she said").
The poem then slows again nearly to a halt as the words
" 'Just that I see'" embody in their cadence the husband's painful, still very reticent recognition of what he
has known "always," but refuses to name (to acknowledge openly) either to himself or to his wife.

These lines are metrically and spatially doing
something that is left unsaid throughout the poem.
What is metrically a single line of (roughly) iambic pen-

tameter verse (" 'What is it—what?' she said./'Just that
I see'" is broken in two on the page, thus allowing the
reader to "see" in the spatial configuration of the lines
what neither husband nor wife can see. The couple is as
much a single unit in their grief and fear as are these
lines a single unit of pentametric verse; the couple, at
the same time, is as divided as the line is spatially sev-
ered (and configured like descending stairs) on the
page and rhythmically broken in its cadence.

It must be clear from the foregoing discussion of
the opening of "Home Burial" that there are two ordinary words and an equally ordinary phrase that are criti-
cally important to the success of this passage. The use of
the word "some" to describe a fear has enormous power
not only to capture the depth and mystery of the familiar, but also to bring to life in the language the struggle
with seeing and knowing. The phrase "to gain time"
manages in a highly condensed way to convey the experience of a person lurching ahead and lagging behind
himself, of attempting to (and being unwilling to) give
words and names to feelings, perceptions, and events
that he fears will make them unbearably real and final.
And, to my mind, the most interesting and moving of
the three, the use of the word "always" (echoing and
then dying in the silent cavity that follows it). The effect
created is that of an experience of timelessness in which
there is no past and no future, only the feeling of
"always." The entire opening passage seems to spread
out forward and backward from the word "always" as if
the lines revolve around this word as a wheel revolves

around a hub. These are ordinary words creating extraordinary effects in language. "No forms [of language] are more engrossing, comforting, staying than those lesser ones we throw off, like vortex rings of smoke . . ." (Frost 1935, p. 740). About a hundred lines later, the poem as a whole ends with a dash (not a period) thus creating a sense of the poem's falling into endless time and space in which the three voices (that of the husband, of the wife, and of the narrator) echo "always."

III.

"I Could Give All to Time" (Frost 1942e), first published when Frost was 68 years old, is a poem that seems to transform itself from good poetry into great poetry in its final stanza.

I Could Give All to Time

To time it never seems that he is brave
To set himself against the peaks of snow
To lay them level with the running wave,
Nor is he overjoyed when they lie low,
But only grave, comtemplative and grave.

What now is inland shall be ocean isle,
Then eddies playing round a sunken reef
Like the curl at the corner of a smile;
And I could share Time's lack of joy or grief
At such a planetary change of style.

I could give all to Time except—except
What I myself have held. But why declare
The things forbidden that while the Customs slept
I have crossed to Safety with? For I am There,
And what I would not part with I have kept.

The poem opens, of course, with the title, in which the speaker is apparently giving himself over to Time, but the word "could" is conditional in a way that leaves open the questions, "If what?" "Under what circumstances?" In the first stanza there is a wry personification of time and a "tribute" to Time's power to lay low "peaks of snow." What is interesting here is the question of who the speaker is, that is, in what relation does the speaker stand to what he is saying? There is a quality of ironic detachment to the voice of the speaker. The word "brave" ending the first line of the stanza has a humorous, almost condescending quality; the word as it is used here has something of the sound of a parent congratulating a child for not crying in the dentist's office. The pun on the word "grave" in the final line of the stanza feels intentionally heavy-handed, particularly when it is repeated "in case the reader did not get it the first time."

The voice in the first three lines of the second stanza feels a bit less removed. The simile comparing "eddies playing round a sunken reef" to "the curl at the corner of a smile" evokes a feeling of bemused acceptance of the erosive power of Time and even contains an acknowledgment of the beauty that the passage of

time may inadvertently create. But, in the final two
lines of the stanza, the whimsical tone seems to take on
a slightly sardonic edge as the speaker refers to "Time's
lack of joy or grief" in response to "planetary change of
style." At this point in the poem it is not at all clear
whether the poem aspires to be anything more than a
clever, well-crafted piece in which there is dry irony in
the fact that Time will do what it will whether or not
one shares in its "lack of joy or grief."

The final stanza begins with the words, "I could
give all to Time" which returns us (for the third time)
to the interesting ambiguity of the word "could" that
from the outset, has been hanging over the poem like
an unresolved musical chord. In the space (of time
and place) between the words "except—except" the
poem seems to "break open" with the sound and feel
of the cracking of the speaker's (and the reader's)
voice over-filled with emotion. The breaking of the
line just before its final word creates an effect in which
the second "except" seems to have been released from
its connection with all that precedes it and to fluidly,
but forcefully "pour over" the edge of the line into the
second line of the stanza. In this way, there is in the
movement of the language itself a sense of the over-
flowing of a boundary after a long period of confine-
ment. (The enjambment[4] of each of the first three
lines of the final stanza contributes to the sense of

---

4. "Enjambment" is the continuation of the end of a line of
poetry into the next without a pause.

strong forward movement.) In contrast to the first two stanzas, the tone in the first line-and-a-half of the final stanza is one of determined (perhaps even quietly joyful) defiance. What is being withheld from time is not simply "what I have held" but "what I myself have held." The word "held" locates the speaking voice squarely in the physical world of felt, palpable things and people (and, by metaphorical extension, the world of intensely felt emotions, feelings, ideas, and beliefs). The speaking voice is that of a man passionately laying claim to what is most sacred to him. At this point in the poem we are very far from the rather aloof cosmological irony conveyed by such words as "planetary change of style."

A passionate voice in the first person is a rare event in Frost's poetry. He regularly shies away from such a display by mixing passion with irony and wit (as in the opening two stanzas of this poem). The poem itself is a risk being taken by the poet in the very act of speaking in a passionate, first-person voice (outside of the protective cover of irony, wit, ambiguity, and the like); the poem could easily degenerate into sophomoric sentimentality and self-aggrandizement. (Few poets have more assiduously guarded against such a development than did Frost in his prime.)

The poem is not "about" the things held most sacred or even "about" the feeling of holding something sacred. The poem *is* what is held most sacred. What it is that makes poetry most sacred is *shown* to us in the experience of "saying" the lines. How could it be otherwise? It is poetry, not a description of poetry, that is held sacred.

The voice having "cracked" and the risk having been taken in allowing passion to be heard and felt in the first person voice of the speaker, the ground is laid for the elegant metaphor that follows:

> But why declare
> The things forbidden that while the Customs slept
> I have crossed to Safety with? For I am There,
> And what I would not part with I have kept.

There is a lyricism to the final stanza (after it "breaks open") that allows us to experience "what I myself have held." What has been withheld from Time, what has been kept alive through the entirety of the speaker's life despite the "weathering" effects of age and loss (wryly alluded to in the first two stanzas) is the making of poetry. At this point, the ironic, detached tone of the first two stanzas is retrospectively transformed a bit as it is experienced as a false bravado that masks a sadness the speaker feels for what has been lost in the course of life.

In the final stanza, the imagery too has shifted from a (somewhat hackneyed) personification of Time as leveler of mountains, to Time (age) as the sleeping customs official past whom the speaker, undetected, carries what is most important to him. The imagery is not only less abstract, it is idiosyncratic, a personal creation that is alive and breathes in the tempo of the music of the words. For example, there is in the third line of the last stanza an extra unstressed syllable that slows the pace of the line and helps to create in the language the sense of caution and danger as the figure in the metaphor quietly slips past the sleeping Customs officer. In the following line, the sentence somewhat awkwardly ends midline with a preposition: "I have crossed to safety with." The sound of the words, with their own imperfect tempo, contributes to the creation of a sense of personal time (ordinary and yet immensely powerful) that replaces the impersonal Time that occupies the first two stanzas. Time, deeply personal time, that is being created in the language of the final stanza is the time with which we struggle in our efforts to remain genuinely alive and not simply living. Although time is by no means defeated in this poem, the rhythms and cadences of the poem are themselves evidence that a poem, a poet, a reader of poetry might "do something with time" when using it to create the tempos of music or poetry or speech or the tempo of the shape of a life.

To borrow from William James (1890, pp. 245–246), the opening part of the final stanza might be thought of as the creation/expression of a "feeling of but" ("But why declare the things forbidden") that becomes in the closing lines of the poem as "feeling of for" and a "feeling of with."

> For I am There,
> And what I would not part with I have kept.

The feeling of "with" that is created in these final lines of the poem is much quieter than what precedes it. There is a sense that as the speaker has aged (and as the poem has been read), a great deal, but not everything has been lost: "And what I would not part with I have kept." The "feeling of with" carries a sense of a calm, but vital connection with, as opposed to a triumph over, time. There can be no triumphs when it comes to time.

The three Frost poems that I have discussed differ greatly from one another in their form and the aspect of the human experience that each addresses. And yet there is a powerful unity that underlies their differences. Each of these poems (or rather the reader's experience of each poem) *is* the living event that the poem addresses, whether that be a particular experience of the love of making and listening to poetry, or the struggle for and against words to bear witness to unspeakable experience, or the effort to keep alive in oneself what is held most sacred over the course of a life. In each instance, the poem is not about an experience; the life of the poem is the experience.

References

Altman, L. (1975). *The Dream in Psychoanalysis*. New York: International Universities Press.

———— (1976). Discussion of Epstein (1976). *Journal of the Philadelphia Association for Psychoanalysis* 3: 58–59.

Ammons, A. R. (1968). A poem is a walk. *Epoch* 28: 114–119.

Balint, M. (1968). *The Basic Fault*. London: Tavistock.

Baranger, M. (1993). The mind of the analyst: from listening to interpretation. *International Journal of Psycho-Analysis* 74: 15–24.

Bion, W. R. (1959). Attacks on linking. *International Journal of Psycho-Analysis* 40: 308–315.

———— (1962a). *Learning from Experience*. New York: Basic Books.

———— (1962b). A theory of thinking. In *Second Thoughts*. New York: Jason Aronson, 1967, pp. 110–119.

———— (1967). Notes on memory and desire. In *Melanie Klein Today, Vol. 2, Mainly Practice*, ed. E. Spillius. London: Routledge, 1988, pp. 17–21.

———— (1978). *Four Discussions with W.R. Bion*. Perthshire, Scotland: Clunie Press

Blechner, M. (1995). The patient's dreams and the countertransference. *Psychoanalytic Dialogues* 5: 1–26.

Bollas, C. (1987). *The Shadow of the Object: Psychoanalysis of the Unthought Known*. New York: Columbia University Press.

Bonime, W. (1962). *The Clinical Use of Dreams*. New York: Basic Books.

Borges, J. L. (1960). The other tiger. In *Jorge Luis Borges: Selected Poems 1923–1967*, trans. and ed. N.T. di Giovanni. New York: Delta, 1968, pp. 129–131.

Boyer, L. B. (1988). Thinking of the interview as if it were a dream. *Contemporary Psychoanalysis* 24: 275–281.

———— (1992). Roles played by music as revealed during countertransference facilitated transference regression. *International Journal of Psycho-Analysis* 73: 55–70.

Britton, R. (1989). The missing link: parental sexuality in the Oedipus complex. In *The Oedipus Complex Today: Clinical Implications*, ed. J. Steiner. London: Karnac, pp. 83–102.

Brodsky, J. (1995a). How to read a book. In *On Grief and Reason: Essays*. New York: Farrar, Straus and Giroux, pp. 96–103.

———— (1995b) On grief and reason. In *On Grief and Reason: Essays*. New York: Farrar, Straus and Giroux, pp. 223–266.

Brower, R. (1951). *The Fields of Light*. New York: Oxford University Press.

———— (1968). *Alexander Pope: The Poetry of Allusion*. New York: Oxford University Press.

Casement, P. (1985). *Learning from the Patient*. New York: Guilford.

Chasseguet–Smirgel, J. (1984). *Creativity and Perversion*. New York: Norton.

Coltart, N. (1986). "Slouching towards Bethlehem" . . . or thinking the unthinkable in psychoanalysis. In *British School of Psychoanalysis: The Independent Tradition*, ed. G. Kohon. New Haven, CT: Yale University Press, pp. 185–199.

———— (1991). The silent patient. *Psychoanalytic Dialogues* 1: 439–454.

Duncan, R. (1960). Often I am permitted to return to a meadow. In *Robert Duncan: Selected Poems*, ed. R. Bertholf. New York: New Directions, 1993, p. 44.

Eliot, T. S. (1921). The metaphysical poets. In *Selected Essays*. New York: Harcourt, Brace and World, 1932, pp. 241–250.

Emerson, R. W. (1841). Art. In *Selected Writings*, ed. B. Atkinson. New York: Random House, 1950, pp. 305–315.

Epstein, G. (1976). A note on a semantic confusion in the fundamental rule of psychoanalysis. *Journal of the Philadelphia Association for Psychoanalysis* 3: 54–57.

Etchegoyen, H. (1991). *The Fundamentals of Psychoanalytic Technique*. London: Karnac.

Faulkner, W. (1946). Appendix. *The Sound and the Fury*. New York: Modern Library, pp. 3–22.

Fenichel, O. (1941). *Problems of Psychoanalytic Technique*. New York: Psychoanalytic Quarterly.

Flannery, J. (1979). Dimensions of a single word-association in the analyst's reverie. *International Journal of Psycho-Analysis* 60: 217–224.

Frank, A. (1995). The couch, the psychoanalytic process, and psychic change: a case study. In *Psychoanalytic Inquiry* 15: 324–337.

Frayn, D. (1987). An analyst's regressive reverie: a response to the analysand's illness. *International Journal of Psycho-Analysis* 68: 271–278.

French, T. and Fromm, E. (1964). *Dream Interpretation: A New Approach*. Madison, CT: International Universities Press.

Freud, S. (1897). Extracts from Fliess papers, Draft M, May 2, 1897. *Standard Edition* 1.

——— (1900). *The Interpretation of Dreams. Standard Edition* 4/5.

——— (1911-15). Papers on technique. *Standard Edition* 12.

——— (1912). Recommendations to physicians practising psychoanalysis. *Standard Edition* 12.

———— (1913). On beginning the treatment. *Standard Edition* 12.

———— (1914). On the history of the psycho-analytic movement. *Standard Edition* 14.

———— (1915). The unconscious. *Standard Edition* 14.

———— (1920). *Beyond the Pleasure Principle. Standard Edition* 18.

———— (1923a). Two encyclopaedia articles. *Standard Edition* 18.

———— (1923b). Remarks on theory and practice of dream-interpretation. *Standard Edition* 19.

———— (1927). Fetishism. *Standard Edition* 21.

Frost, R. (1913). Letter to John T. Bartlett, July 4, 1913. In *Selected Letters of Robert Frost*, ed. L. Thompson. New York: Holt, Rinehart and Winston, 1964, pp. 79–81.

———— (1914a). Letter to John T. Bartlett, February 22, 1914. In *Robert Frost: Collected Poems, Prose and Plays*, ed. R. Poirier and M. Richardson. New York: Library of America, 1995, pp. 673–679.

———— (1914b). Home burial. In *Robert Frost: Collected Poems, Prose and Plays*, ed. R. Poirier and M. Richardson. New York: Library of America, 1995, pp. 55–58.

———— (1915). 'The imagining ear.' In *Robert Frost: Collected Poems, Prose and Plays*, ed. R. Poirier and M. Richardson. New York: Library of America, 1995, pp. 687–689.

———— (1917). Letter to Louis Untermeyer. In *Frost: A Literary Life Reconsidered*, W. Pritchard. Amherst, MA: University of Massachusetts Press, 1984, pp. 126–127.

———— (1918). The unmade word. In *Robert Frost: Collected Poems, Prose and Plays*, ed. R. Poirier and M. Richardson. New York: Library of America, 1995, pp. 694–697.

———— (1923). Some definitions. In *Robert Frost: Collected Poems, Prose and Plays*, ed. R. Poirier and M. Richardson. New York: Library of America, 1995, p. 701.

———— (1929). Preface. *A Way Out.* In *Robert Frost: Collected Poems, Prose and Plays*, ed. R. Poirier and M. Richardson. New York: Library of America, 1995, p. 713.

────── (1935). Letter to "The Amherst Student." In *Robert Frost: Collected Poems, Prose and Plays*, ed. R. Poirier and M. Richardson. New York: Library of America, 1995, p. 739–740.

────── (1936). Letter to L. W. Payne, Jr., 12 March 1936. In *Selected Letters of Robert Frost*, ed. L. Thompson. New York: Holt, Rinehart and Winston, 1964, pp. 426–427.

────── (1939). The figure a poem makes. In *Robert Frost: Collected Poems, Prose and Plays*, ed. R. Poirier and M. Richardson. New York: Library of America, 1995, pp. 776–778.

────── (1942a). Carpe diem. In *Robert Frost: Collected Poems, Prose and Plays*, ed. R. Poirier and M. Richardson. New York: Library of America, 1995, p. 305.

────── (1942b). The most of it. In *Robert Frost: Collected Poems, Prose and Plays*, ed. R. Poirier and M. Richardson. New York: Library of America, 1995, p. 307.

────── (1942c). The silken tent. In *Robert Frost: Collected Poems, Prose and Plays*, ed. R. Poirier and M. Richardson. New York: Library of America, 1995, p. 301.

────── (1942d). Beeches. In *Robert Frost: Collected Poems, Prose and Plays*, ed. R. Poirier and M. Richardson. New York: Library of America, 1995, p. 302.

────── (1942e). I could give all to time. In *Robert Frost: Collected Poems, Prose and Plays*, ed. R. Poirier and M. Richardson. New York: Library of America, 1995, pp. 304–305.

────── (1962). On extravagance: a talk. In *Robert Frost: Collected Poems, Prose and Plays*, ed. R. Poirier and M. Richardson. New York: Library of America, 1995, pp. 902–926.

Gaddini, E. (1982). Early defensive phantasies and the psychoanalytic process. In *A Psychoanalytic Theory of Infantile Experience: Conceptual and Clinical Reflections*, ed. A. Limentani. London: Routledge, 1992, pp. 142–153.

Garma, A. (1966). *The Psychoanalysis of Dreams*. Chicago: Quadrangle Books.

Goethe, J. W. (1808). Faust I and II. In *Goethe: The Collected Works, Vol. 2.*, ed. and trans. S. Atkins. Princeton: Princeton University Press, 1984.

Goldberger, M. (1995). The couch as defense and potential for enactment. *Psychoanalytic Quarterly* 63: 23–42.

Gray, P. (1992). Memory as resistance, and the telling of a dream. *Journal of the American Psychoanalytic Association* 40: 307–326.

——— (1994). *The Ego and the Analysis of Defense.* Northvale, NJ: Jason Aronson.

Green, A. (1975). The analyst, symbolisation and absence in the analytic setting (On changes in analytic practice and analytic experience). *International Journal of Psycho-Analysis* 56: 1–22.

——— (1983). The dead mother. In *On Private Madness.* Madison, CT: International Universities Press, 1986, pp. 142–173.

——— (1987). La capacité de rêverie et le myth étiologique. *Revue Française de Psychanalyse* 51: 1299–1315.

Greenson, R. (1967). *The Technique and Practice of Psychoanalysis, Volume 1.* New York: International Universities Press.

——— (1971). Panel. The basic rule: free association–a reconsideration. Reporter, H. Seidenberger, *Journal of the American Psychoanalytic Association* 19: 98–109.

Grotstein, J. (1979). Who is the dreamer who dreams the dream and who is the dreamer who understands it? *Contemporary Psychoanalysis* 15: 110–169.

——— (1995). A reassessment of the couch in psychoanalysis. *Psychoanalytic Inquiry* 15: 396–405.

Isakower, O. (1938). A contribution to the psychopathology of phenomena related to falling asleep. *International Journal of Psycho-Analysis* 19: 331–335.

——— (1963). Minutes of faculty meeting, New York Psychoanalytic Institute, Nov. 20.

Jacobson, J. (1995). The analytic couch: facilitator or sine qua non? *Psychoanalytic Inquiry* 15: 304–313.

James, H. (1881). *The Portrait of a Lady*. Boston: Houghton Mifflin, 1963.

——— (1884). The art of fiction. In *Henry James: Literary Criticism. Vol 1: Essays on Literature, American Writers, English Writers*. New York: Library of America, 1984, pp. 44–65.

James, W. (1890). *Principles of Psychology, Vol. 1.*, ed. P. Smith. New York: Dover, 1950.

Jarrell, R. (1953). *Poetry and the Age*. New York: Vintage, 1955.

Joseph, B. (1975). The patient who is difficult to reach. In *Psychic Equilibrium and Psychic Change*. ed. M. Feldman and E. B. Spillius. New York: Routledge, 1989, pp. 75–87.

——— (1982). Addiction to near death. *International Journal of Psycho-Analysis* 63: 449–456.

——— (1985). Transference: the total situation. *International Journal of Psycho-Analysis* 66: 447–454.

——— (1994). 'Where there is no vision . . .' from sexualization to sexuality. Presented at the San Francisco Psychoanalytic Institute, San Francisco, April, 1994.

Khan, M. M. R. (1976). Beyond the dreaming experience. In *Hidden Selves: Between Theory and Practice in Psychoanalysis*. Madison, CT: International Universities Press, 1983, pp. 42 -51.

——— (1979). *Alienation in Perversions*. New York: International Universities Press.

Klein, M. (1926). Psychological principles of infant analysis. In *Contributions to Psycho-Analysis, 1921–1945*. London: Hogarth, 1968, pp. 140–151.

——— (1928). Early stages of the Oedipus conflict. In *Contributions to Psycho-Analysis, 1921–1945*. London: Hogarth, 1968, pp. 202–214.

——— (1952). The origins of transference. In *Envy and Gratitude and Other Works, 1946–1963*. New York: Delacorte, 1975, pp. 48–56.

Klein, S. (1980). Autistic phenomena in neurotic patients. *International Journal of Psycho-Analysis* 61: 395–401.

Lawrence, D. H. (1919). Foreword. *Women in Love*. New York: Modern Library, 1950.

Leavis, F. R. (1947). *Revaluation*. New York: Norton.

Lebovici, S. (1987). Le psychanalyste et "le capacité à la rêverie de la mère." *Revue Française de Psychanalyse* 51: 1317–1345.

Lewin, B. (1950). *The Psychoanalysis of Elation*. New York: The Psychoanalytic Quarterly Press.

Lichtenberg, J. (1995). Forty-five years of psychoanalytic experience on, behind, and without the couch. *Psychoanalytic Inquiry* 15: 280–293.

Lichtenberg, J. and Galler, F. (1987). The fundamental rule: a study of current usage. *Journal of the American Psychoanalytic Association* 35: 45–76.

Loewald, H. (1986). Transference-countertransference. *Journal of the American Psychoanalytic Association* 34: 275–287.

Malcolm, R. (1970) The mirror: a perverse sexual phantasy in a woman seen as a defence against a psychotic breakdown. In *Melanie Klein Today, Vol. 2: Mainly Practice*, ed. E. Spillius. Routledge: New York, 1988, pp. 115–137.

────── (1995). The three "W's": what, where and when: the rationale of interpretation. *International Journal of Psycho-Analysis* 76: 447–456.

McDougall, J, (1978). The primal scene and the perverse scenario. In *Plea for a Measure of Abnormality*. New York: International Universities Press, 1980, pp. 53–86.

────── (1986). Identifications, neoneeds and neosexualities. *International Journal of Psycho-Analysis* 67: 19–31.

Meares, R. (1993). *The Metaphor of Play*. Northvale, NJ: Jason Aronson.

Meltzer, D. (1973). *Sexual States of Mind*. Perthshire, Scotland: Clunie Press.

Mitchell, S. (1993). *Hope and Dread in Psychoanalysis*. New York: Basic Books.

Musil, R. (1924). *Five Women*, trans. E. Wilkins and E. Kaiser. Boston: Nonpareil Books, 1968.

Ogden, T. (1986). *The Matrix of the Mind: Object Relations and the Psychoanalytic Dialogue.* Northvale, NJ: Jason Aronson/ London: Karnac.

———— (1988a). Misrecognitions and the fear of not knowing. *Psychoanalytic Quarterly* 57: 643–666.

———— (1988b). On the dialectical structure of experience: some clinical and theoretical implications. *Contemporary Psychoanalysis* 24: 17–45.

———— (1989a). On the concept of an autistic-contiguous position. *International Journal of Psycho-Analysis* 70: 127–140.

———— (1989b). *The Primitive Edge of Experience.* Northvale, NJ: Jason Aronson/London: Karnac.

———— (1991a). Analysing the matrix of transference. *International Journal of Psycho-Analysis* 72: 593–605.

———— (1991b). Some theoretical comments on personal isolation. *Psychoanalytic Dialogues* 1: 377–390.

———— (1992a). The dialectically constituted/decentred subject of psychoanalysis. I. The Freudian subject. *International Journal of Psycho-Analysis* 73: 517–526.

———— (1992b). The dialectically constituted/decentred subject of psychoanalysis. II. The contributions of Klein and Winnicott. *International Journal of Psycho-Analysis* 73: 613–626.

———— (1994a). The analytic third–working with intersubjective clinical facts. *The International Journal of Psycho-Analysis* 75: 3–20.

———— (1994b). The concept of interpretive action. *Psychoanalytic Quarterly* 63: 219–245.

———— (1994c). Indentificação projectiva e o terceiro subjugador. *Revista de Psicanálise de Sociedade Psicanalítica de Porto Alegre* 2: 153–162. (Published in English as "Projective Identification and the Subjugating Third." In *Subjects of Analysis.* Northvale, NJ: Jason Aronson, 1994, pp. 97–106.)

———— (1994d). *Subjects of Analysis.* Northvale, NJ: Jason Aronson/London: Karnac.

O'Shaughnessy, E. (1989). The invisible Oedipus complex. In *The Oedipus Complex Today: Clinical Implications*, ed. J. Steiner. London: Karnac, pp. 129–150.

Peltz, R. (1996). The anatomy of impasses and the retrieval of meaning states. Presented at "Discussions for Clinicians," San Francisco Psychoanalytic Institute, Oct. 7.

Phillips, A. (1996). *Terrors and Experts*. Cambridge: Harvard University Press.

Poirier, R. (1977). *Robert Frost: The Work of Knowing*. New York: Oxford University Press.

——— (1992). *Poetry and Pragmatism*. Cambridge, MA: Harvard University Press.

Pontalis, J. B. (1977). Between the dream as object and the dream-text. In *Frontiers in Psychoanalysis: Between the Dream and Psychic Pain*. Madison, CT: International Universities Press, pp. 23–55.

Pritchard, W. (1984). *Frost: A Literary Life Reconsidered*. Amherst, MA: University of Massachusetts Press.

——— (1991). Ear training. In *Playing it by Ear: Literary Essays and Reviews*. Amherst, MA: University of Massachusetts Press, 1994, pp. 3–18.

Rangell, L. (1987). Historical perspectives and current status of the interpretation of dreams in clinical work. In *The Interpretation of Dreams in Clinical Work*, ed. A. Rothstein. Madison, CT: International Universities Press, pp. 3–24.

Rilke, R. M. (1904). Letters. In *Rilke on Love and Other Difficulties*, trans. J. J. L. Mood. New York: Norton, 1975, p. 27.

Sandler, J. (1976). Dreams, unconscious fantasies and 'identity of perception.' *International Review of Psycho-Analysis* 3: 33–42.

Schafer, R. (1994). *Retelling a Life: Narration and Dialogue in Psychoanalysis*. New York: Basic Books.

Searles, H. (1975). The patient as therapist to the analyst. In *Tactics and Techniques in Psychoanalytic Therapy, Vol. 2*, ed. P. L. Giovacchini. New York: Jason Aronson, pp. 95–151.

Segal, H. (1991). *Dream, Phantasy and Art*. London: Tavistock/ Routledge.

Sharpe, E. (1937). *Dream Analysis*. London: Hogarth Press, 1949.

Spillius, E. B. (1995). Kleinian perspectives on transference. Presented at the San Francisco Psychoanalytic Institute, September, 1995.

Steiner, J. (1985). Turning a blind eye: the cover-up for Oedipus. *International Review of Psycho-Analysis* 12: 161–172.

Stevens, W. (1947). The creations of sound. In *The Collected Poems of Wallace Stevens*. New York: Knopf, 1967.

Stewart, H. (1977). Problems of management in the analysis of a hallucinating hysteric. *International Journal of Psycho-Analysis* 38: 67–76.

Strachey, J. (1934). The nature of the therapeutic action of psychoanalysis. *International Journal of Psycho-Analysis* 15: 127–159.

Symington, N. (1983). The analyst's act of freedom as agent of therapeutic change. *International Review of Psycho-Analysis* 10: 283–291.

Tustin, F. (1980). Autistic objects. *International Review of Psycho-Analysis* 7: 27–40.

——— (1984). Autistic shapes. *International Review of Psycho-Analysis* 11: 279–290.

Whitman, R., Kramer, M., and Baldridge, B. (1969). Dreams about the patient. *Journal of the American Psychoanalytic Association* 17: 702–727.

Whitman, W. (1871). Democratic vistas. In *Whitman: Poetry and Prose*. New York: Library of America, 1982, pp. 929–994.

Winnicott, D. W. (1947). Hate in the countertransference. In *Through Paediatrics to Psycho-Analysis*. New York: Basic Books, 1975, pp. 194–203.

——— (1951). Transitional objects and transitional phenomena. In *Playing and Reality*. New York: Basic Books, 1971, pp. 1–25.

———— (1960). The theory of the parent-infant relationship. In *The Maturational Processes and the Facilitating Environment.* New York: International Universities Press, 1965, pp. 37–55.

———— (1963). Communicating and not communicating leading to a study of certain opposites. In *The Maturational Processes and the Facilitating Environment.* New York: International Universities Press, 1965, pp. 179–192.

———— (1971a). Playing: a theoretical statement. In *Playing and Reality.* New York: Basic Books, pp. 38–52.

———— (1971b). *Playing and Reality.* New York: Basic Books.

———— (1971c). The place where we live. In *Playing and Reality.* New York: Basic Books, pp. 104–110.

———— (1971d). Introduction. In *Playing and Reality.* New York: Basic Books, pp. xii–xiii.

———— (1971e). Playing: creative activity and the search for the self. In *Playing and Reality.* New York: Basic Books, pp. 53–64.

———— (1974). Fear of breakdown. *International Review of Psycho-Analysis* 1: 103–107.

Zweibel, R. (1985). The countertransference dream. *International Review of Psycho-Analysis* 12: 87–99.

Index